AF541075

Coalition Politics in North East India

B. Pakem

2020

Regency Publications
A Division of
Astral International Pvt. Ltd.
New Delhi – 110 002

First Published, 1999

Reprinted, 2020

ISBN: 9788186030196

Disclaimer:

Every possible effort has been made to ensure that the information contained in this book is accurate at the time of going to press, and the publisher and author cannot accept responsibility for any errors or omissions, however caused. No responsibility for loss or damage occasioned to any person acting, or refraining from action, as a result of the material in this publication can be accepted by the editor, the publisher or the author. The Publisher is not associated with any product or vendor mentioned in the book. The contents of this work are intended to further general scientific research, understanding and discussion only. Readers should consult with a specialist where appropriate.

Every effort has been made to trace the owners of copyright material used in this book, if any. The author and the publisher will be grateful for any omission brought to their notice for acknowledgement in the future editions of the book.

Published by : **Regency Publications**
A Division of
Astral International Pvt. Ltd.
– ISO 9001:2015 Certified Company –
4736/23, Ansari Road, Darya Ganj
New Delhi-110 002
Ph. 011-43549197, 23278134
E-mail: info@astralint.com
Website: www.astralint.com

Digitally Printed at : **Replika Press Pvt. Ltd.**

Dedicated to My Mother
Ka Kwinsibon Pakem (1912–1998)

PREFACE

In recent years, coalition politics has attracted the attention of public leaders, policy-makers, administrators, social scientists and the citizens at large. This attention is due mainly to the anxiety arising out of the instability of coalition governments in our country. The people, in general, would welcome any governmental set up provided political stability is ensured. But, of late, public leaders have almost lost their credibility, in the eyes of the people, precisely because of their failures to bring back stable governments. The public leaders, on their part, try to defend themselves by shifting the responsibility to the fractured verdict of the people at the hustings.

It may be true that both the people and their leaders are equally responsible for such a political situation. However, public leaders have more responsibility in respecting the verdict of the people at the polls by trying to experiment with coalition politics on a sound basis. But, it so happened that, more often than not, the public leaders taking advantage of the hung parliament and the hung State Assemblies have resorted to unhealthy practices of horse-trading and floor crossing, notwithstanding the Tenth Schedule to the Constitution of India. It is indeed a very sad commentary on the current state of political affairs in our country in general and in North-East India in particular.

When I was invited by Prof. J.P. Singh, Honorary Director of the North-Eastern Regional Centre of the Indian Council of Social Science Research to deliver the first Rajiv Gandhi Memorial Lectures under the auspices of the Rajiv Gandhi Foundation, I felt very much highly privileged for the honour bestowed upon me. Having accepted the assignment what has immediately come to my mind is to speak on coalition politics in North East India. I feel that it is important to know about the political situation in the region in the context of recent highly competitive politics which has led to so many coalition experiments in regional and sub-regional statecraft. The dearth of source materials, however, has limited my lectures only to State Legislative Assembly level. Hence, in these lectures, I have left out of consideration on the processes of coalition politics at the other levels like the municipalities, other local self-government institutions, panchayats, autonomous district councils, autonomous regional councils, and village councils. Even at the State Assembly level, more primary sources are yet to be tapped. Due to the time constraint within which I have to complete the preparation for these lectures, I cannot but heavily depend on secondary sources. But, all the same, these sources would indicate the trend towards the continuation of coalition politics at the State level given the present system of representative government under the Indian Constitution.

The three lectures have been organised to cover: (1) A theoretical consideration on coalition politics, (2) coalition politics during the British period, and (3) coalition politics since India's Independence. My main finding through these lectures is that what has been so far experimented on coalition politics in the region is not so much successful due to a number of problems. These problems cover a wider range of issues like insurgency activities, ethnic movements, student movements, community consideration rather than consideration of political ideology in coalition politics, and an entrenched regionalism leading to the regionalisation of Indian Government and politics. Over and above these issues it must be stressed that at the national level there has been no institutionalisation of coalition politics in North-East India either. I do believe that through the process of such institutionalisation, coalition politics in the region may become stable and successful in future.

I must acknowledge my gratefulness to the authorities of the North Eastern Regional Centre of the Indian Council of Social Science Research and of the Rajiv Gandhi Foundation for having given me this opportunity to delve into this important aspect of the political activities in the seven sister States of North East India. In the preparation of these lectures, I must put on record my appreciation of the help and assistance extended to me by Dr. L. Pathak, Librarian of the North-Eastern Hill University and the members of his staff for sparing no pain in providing me with the source materials from the NEHU, Central Library. My thanks also go to Sarvasri Dhiraj Chakravorty, Fullmoon Kharmihpen and Ashish Kumar Dhar as well as to the Staff of the Publication wing of NEHU for their generous secretarial assistance.

Shillong
November 26, 1998

B. Pakem

CONTENTS

1

THEORETICAL CONSIDERATION

SECTION 1: GENESIS OF COALITIONS

In ancient time, coalitions were practised by States and Governments both in war and politics. Consider the Peloponnesian war among the Greek City States under the Athenian Ionic League and the Spartan Doric League during 431–404 B.C.[1] or the Roman Triumvirate under Antony, Cicero and Octovian after Julius Caeser's assassination in 44. B.C.[2] In ancient India (3100 B.C., or 1400 B.C., or 900 B.C.) too, there were coalitions during the Mahabharata, an epic war where a number of *Janapadas* were aligning themselves either with the Kauravas or with the Pandavas.[3] Even ancient Assam or Pragjyotishpur (Kamrup) of North-East India was joining that Great Epic War with its King, Bhagadatta who was killed by the Pandavas at Kurukshetra.[4] Not only in war but also in politics the principle of coalition was involved in the Peloponnesian War. The Greek City States joining the Ionian League was essentially due to their love for the Athenian democracy while those States under the Doric League were supporting the political ideology of oligarchy of Sparta.[5]

To cut the story short, in our own century we have witnessed the two Great World Wars. The First World War (1914–18) was fought between the Allied Powers coalition and the Central Powers coalition. Similarly, the Second World War (1939–45) was fought between the Allied Powers coalition and the Axis Powers coalition. Finally, the Cold War (1945–90) was a war between the Western Bloc coalition under the leadership of the United States and the Communist Bloc coalition under the leadership of the Soviet Union. And today in the general economic competition we have a sort of a coalition among the G-7 of the Developed North and of the G-15 of the Developing South; or in the Nuclear Club we also have the coalition partners of the pro-Non-Profileration and the coalition partners of the anti-Non-Profileration. In one word, we may perhaps apply the concept of coalition of any game of power struggle whether at the international, national, regional or sub-regional levels.

In India, the national political situation today is facing a period of instability arising out of no single party getting a clear majority in forming the government. At the regional level also many States are facing similar situations. One may like it or not, coalition politics has become an essential feature of present day Indian democracy. Subhas C. Kashyap in his *The Politics of Power: Defections and State Politics in India* (1975) comments in the context of the political scenario ever since 1967 that, "there could be little escape from an era of coalition governments".[6] He also refers to the views of many political leaders about the inevitability of coalition politics in the country. Excepting the Prime Minister, Indira Gandhi and Nijalingappa, President of the Indian National Congress who were not in favour of coalition governments at that time, many leaders accepted it as a *fait accompli*. Sri. N.G. Ranga of the Swatantra Party was of the view that there should be "coalition governments by non-communist democratic parties".[7] Ram Gopal, Vice-President of the Bhartiya Kranti Dal considered coalition as "inevitable at the present stage of Indian democracy" [8] S.N. Dwivedi of the Praja Socialist Party called the political situation of the day as "a decade of coalition governments".[9]

The Jan Sangh President, Atal Behari Vajpayee was of the opinion that the formation of coalition governments was a political necessity or "compulsion".[10] The Deputy Prime Minister Morarji Desai did not rule out the possibility of other parties entering into a coalition government with the Congress Party provided the other parties in such a coalition should be prepared to accept and fall in line substantially with the Congress Programmes.[11] Contrary to popular beliefs, however, Dayabhai Patel of the Swatantra Party while participating in the Parliamentary Committee for Curbing Defection thought that "the growth of more and more coalitions may help check defection."[12]

These were some of the political views and opinions of the representative cross-sections of the different political parties during the early period of coalition politics in the country. Now, before we proceed further in our consideration of the theoretical aspects of the subject matter let us briefly discuss on what is actually meant by coalition.

SECTION 2: DEFINITIONS OF COALITION

But what do we really mean when using the term coalition or coalition politics anyway? It is indeed a very difficult task to have a direct and simple response to such a querry. The *Oxford English Dictionary* (1961) gives the meaning of a coalition as a "union, combination, fusion of parties, principles, interests, etc"; and especially in politics it means: "An alliance for combined action of distinct parties, persons, or states, without permanent incorporation into one body".[13] The *Random House of English Language* (1970) defines coalition as "a continuation or alliance, especially a temporary one between persons, factions, states, etc".[14] But dictionary meanings are quite limited in scope when we use the term "coalition" in its technical sense. The *Encyclopaedia of Social Sciences* (1972) has made an attempt to give a technical meaning through social scientists like William H. Riker and William A. Gamson.

Riker writers that: "The word 'coalition' has long been used in ordinary English to refer to a group of people who come together (usually on a temporary basis) to attain some end. Typically, a coalition has been regarded as a parliamentary or political grouping less permanent than a party or faction or an interest group".[15] As differentiated from the ordinary or dictionary meaning of the term coalition, Riker has also added a technical definition of coalition when he says: "Recently, however, the word has acquired a technical significance in social science theories with the elaboration (in the last two decades) of the theory of n-person games",[16] and that the notion of coalition formation is central to this theory, since "coalitions are the characteristic form of social organisation by which the outcomes of such games are determined".[17] Coalition, he asserts, provides a model for the study of decision making ranging from elections, parliaments, committees, cabinets, etc. at the national level; and decision making in wars, diplomatic maneuvers, and internal organisations at the international level. He, therefore, reiterates that: "coalitions are the characteristic form of social organization for political decision making generally".[18]

On the other hand, Gamson uses the word "coalition" to "mean the *joint use of resources to determine the outcome of a decision,* where a resource is some weight such that some critical quantity of it in the control of two or more parties to the decision is both necessary and sufficient to determine its outcome. Participants will be said to be using their resources jointly only if they co-ordinate their deployment of resources with respect to some decision. That is what is meant by saying that they have formed a coalition".[19] These two authors have agreed in their definitions of coalition, at least, in two important aspects, that is, on decision making and games. After a discussion on these two aspects, Gamson comes to a greater precision in his definition of a coalition as "the joint use of resources to determine the outcome of a decision in a mixed-motive situation involving more than two units" [20] Regarding the detailed discussion on decision making and games theories by Riker and Gamson will be separately dealt with in Section 5 below.

Other writers, both Western and Eastern, have more or less agreed with the definitions given by Riker and Gamson. For example, Arend Lijphart in his *Democracy in Plural Societies: A Comparative Exploration* (1989)[21] talks about a "plural society" which is a society divided by what Harry Eckstein calls "segmental cleavages" based on religious, ideological, linguistic, regional, or ethnic nature.[22] This definition implies that segmental cleavages in a plural society are mobilised or organised by political parties, interest groups, media of communication, schools and voluntary associations. But segmental cleavages in plural societies as in the Third World countries are quite different from segmental cleavages in homogenous societies like Britain and France. This finding is based on what is known as the Lewis model where in his *Politics in West Africa* (1965)[23] observes that "plural societies are divided by tribal, religious, linguistic, cultural, economic, and regional differences. Class societies are the essentially homogenous societies but is not a deep cleavage".[24] Hence, "What is good for a class society is bad for a plural society" he concluded.[25] We may recall at this juncture what Ambedkar had said in the Constituent Assembly: "Democracy in India is only top dressing on an Indian soil, which is essentially undemocratic".[26]

It is in this context that Lijphart is speaking about "the consociational model . . . as an alternative to the British model of democracy in the plural societies of the Third World".[27] However, such a consociational model for the Third World countries may not really bridge the differences between the various segments in their respective countries. In fact, "the chances of bridging them by consociational methods are nil or infinitesimally small" [28] It is quite interesting to note that Lijphart while talking about consociational democracy in the plural societies he also refers to the concept of a grand coalition by applying Riker's games theory. But this type of coalition, according to Lijphart "is not realistic . . .except in the most extreme case of a plural society".[29] A more detailed discussion on this aspect will be dealt with in Section 5 below. Here, suffice it to say that Lijphart looks at the possible definition of a coalition on the basis of segmental cleavages in the plural societies.

Among the Indian theoreticians, Rajni Kothari, in 1970, writing on *Politics in India* is more or less convinced that "the country is set on a period of coalitional governments, not only in the States but also at the Centre".[30] But throughout his writing in the book, there was no definition of what coalition is about. True, he uses the terms like the Congress Party being a "grand coalition",[31] or the historical character of the Congress Party "as a coalitional arena",[32] "The coalitional arena of Indian Politics",[33] "coalition of protests" and the traditional style of "coalition-making",[34] yet we have to look for his definition of a coalition. Perhaps, we may surmise about such a definition from his comments on the "powerful built-in resistance to a zero-(sum) game",[35] and his view that: "Demands can be muted by implicit pressures for consensus".[36] In other words, his implicit definition of a coalition refers more to an intra-party coalition rather than on an inter-party coalition, though it also involves the question of governmental coalition as differentiated from a party (intra-party or inter-party) coalition.

It is in the above context that we may appreciate Kothari's comment that while there is a degree of "confrontation" between opposing groups in the Congress Party, yet he is of the opinion that: "A better alternative may be for the formation of a viable coalition of proximate groups, a coalition that provides both governmental stability and the necessary strength for making and enforcing critical decisions".[37] It is also because of this fact that he came to the conclusion: "Democratic Politics are everywhere the politics of coalition making"[38] both at the intra-party and inter-party levels as well as at the governmental level. The ramification of intra-party and inter-party coalitions will be dealt with separately in Sections 3 and 4 respectively.

Other Indian scholars working on the definitions of coalition politics a mention may be made of Harish Khare and E. Sridharan. According to Khare, "coalition politics by definition is a temporary arrangement and sustains itself only if each partner feels, or is made to feel, that its long term interest would not necessarily be compromised, while it also enjoys some temporary benefits".[39] Sridharan, on the other hand, while not referring to the minority—nor oversized—coalitions emphsises the importance of minimum winning coalitions" based on power maximisation theories as against policy based theories. The minimum winning coalition is defined by him "as a coalition in which each party is indispensable to the coalition's winning a simple majority of seats, because in such coalitions each member's share of the pay off is maximized".[40] Thus, any definition of a coalition is somehow connected with theories of coalition. Theories of coalition will be examined in detail in Section 5 below.

Earlier, there was an attempt to indirectly define coalition by some writers like A.R. Desai. In *States and Society in India: Essays in Dissent* (1975), Desai observed that, "the alliances, united fronts and coalitions made upto now basically do not reveal any principled stand by any party. All the parties exhibit cross-opportunism in making alliances, associating with any party or group subserving vote catching and enabling maximum seats in the bargain".[41] Similarly, Raghuveer Singh says that: "In its ordinary usage coalition refers to a group of people who come together to achieve some end, usually or a temporary basis. In politics, it signifies a parliamentary or political grouping of different parties, interest groups or factions formed for making and/or influencing policy-decisions or securing power",[42] Singh's definition seems to have been based on the definition of Riker as reflected in *Encyclopaedia of Social Sciences*.

With the ever increasing number of coalition making and coalition breaking in India, the Indian Institute of Public Administration, New Delhi had organised its Fortieth Annual Conference on October 27,1996 on the theme of "Coalition Government: Experience and Prospects". In his theme paper in the conference, O.P. Minocha also subscribed to the definition of a coalition in these words: "The word 'coalition' generally refers to a group of people who come together (usually on a temporary basis) to obtain some end. Typically, a coalition has been regarded as a parliamentary or political grouping, less permanent than a party or faction or an interest group. Coalition implies co-operation between political parties" [43]

A cursory glance over the above definitions of coalition does not really give us a very satisfactory connotation of what coalition is in the context of North-East Indian Government and politics. The subject matter of this lecture being on coalition politics in North-East politics in North-East India, it is always our quest to find out, from the historical perspective, about the genesis, growth and greening of coalition in the North-East Indian context. Yes, coalition politics remains ever green ever since modern parliamentary democracy was introduced in the region, and there is no sign of its decaying as yet.

But what is coalition in the North-East India perspective? So far, we have no definition. However, our assessment of the political situation in the region is that, historically, coalition is part and parcel of its political processes whether under medieval monarchy, traditional indigenous political system, or modern parliamentary democracy. In a land with so many warring clans, autonomous villages, independent tribes and communities living side by side in a small geographical area, it is but natural that the principle of coalition is inherent in the political system itself. Neither by divine intervention nor by human design, coalition just evolves in the fertile political soil of North-East India.

While in modern parlance, we may talk about intra-party or inter-party coalitions, or segmental cleavages in the political society, simultaneously we may also talk about intra-clan/inter-clan, intra-village/inter-village, and intra-tribal/inter-tribal coalitions while discussing about coalition politics in North-East India. Hence, in this lecture, rather than laying an emphasis of political rivalries as hitherto emphasised by many writers, an emphasis is laid more on political coalitions among different clans, villages, tribes and communities of the region. In this connection, it is worthwhile to ponder over the definition of coalition by Amintore Fanfani, the Former Prime Minister of Italy. While closely perceiving the processes of coalitions in his country, the land of so many coalitions in recent years his definition of coalition "is like marriage in which jealousy is greater than love".[44] Perhaps, presently we can say this much for political coalitions in North-East India too.

SECTION 3: INTRA-PARTY COALITION

When Rajni Kothari expresses himself that the Congress Party in India is a "grand-coalition" he has in mind about the nature of an intra-party coalition of the Congress. The Congress was then leading the opposition movement against the British authorities. He says: "Like any broad oppositional movement it contained within its fold several splint groups ranged over a wide span of ideological and policy perspectives. Thus the Communist Party, the Hindu Mahasabha, and the Socialist Party were all at one time part of the Congress movement. Dissidents from the ruling leadership also often pulled out of the Congress, set up other parties, and often returned to the Congress when the situation had crystallized in their favour".[45] This pattern was inherent in the Congress Party until 1969 when, in the words of Kothari, "there now developed an emphasis on Unity of purpose and a more cohesive team, with a willingness to allow opposing groups to leave the party, and there was less anxiety about party defections".[46]

But the gradual erosion of the Congress since then in the form of Congress (O), Congress (S), Congress (J), etc. made its leaders to think in terms of stopping the exodus from the party by adopting a parliamentary legislation to prevent defection in the Indian legislatures. This only indicates that the Congress cannot afford to remain a mere "Centre" Party but have also to include the rightists and the leftists within its fold. In other words, the Congress is to remain a coalition party, if it has to retain governmental power both at the Centre and in the States. In the words of Riker, the Congress Party was in fact "a coalition of the whole by 1948"[47] and after the 1969 split tried to retain that status.

Prior to 1947 the Congress Party was at the centre stage comprising almost all sections of the Indian society including those from among the minorities and backward castes. But then there were exclusive separate political parties also like the Muslim League, the Scheduled Castes Federation, the Communist Party, the Hindu Mahasabha, and the Indian Princes. In 1948, however, the Congress found itself to be "a coalition of the whole".[48] However, this position was not what the Congress had planned. So, when it found its new power status, the Congress started "increasing the value of their coalition by expelling members and thereby creating a losing side".[49] The Congress started expelling the Hindu Mahasabha after Gandhi's assasination, and eliminated the Communists through police action as in Hyderabad and Manipur.

Inspite of this attempt at eliminating the rightists and the leftists from the Congress fold, factionalism in the party continued. There were then two clearly defined factions in the party. One faction was led by Pandit Jawaharlal Nehru and Jaya Prakash Narayan, and the other by Sardar Vallabhai Patel. The former was broadened as a Socialist group within the Congress and the latter as the Conservative Group. There was also a tussle between the two groups during the life time of Sardar Patel.[50]

The tussle was like a fight to the finish between the two groups. During the period 1948–50 there was the question of who would expel whom. It was said that Sardar Patel being an organisational man had certain advantages. His dislike of the Socialist Group was to the extent that he forbade the use of the word "Congress" from the phrase "Congress Socialist group". Because of this, many socialists left the Congress in 1948 itself.[51]

When a large number of socialists left the Congress, it appeared as if the intra-party coalition was over. In fact, Patel was to take over the Party in 1950 when he got Purushottamdas Tandon from his faction elected as President of the Congress. As a result of this election more followers of Nehru's Socialist Group left the party. The process could not, however, be completed as meanwhile Patel passed away. Nehru though belonging to the Socialist Group and who did not part company with Patel took over the party organisation and forced Tandon to resign. After Tandon's resignation, Nehru took upon himself the Presidentship of the Party as well as running as Head of the Government.[52]

It was from this dual position that Nehru could pursue his secular and socialist objectives and put down the conservative elements in the party. While very few socialists came back to the Congress fold, a large number of the Conservatives left the organisation. The factional struggle reflected the fortune of the party in the First General Elections of 1952 when the Congress secured only 45 per cent of the popular votes. It was reported that the Conservatives had voted for the independent candidates rather than for the Congress candidates. Though the popular votes secured by the Congress won a minority of votes, yet it secured 74 per cent of the parliamentary seats on the basis of the winning candidates "first passing the post." Because of this, the Congress as a party during the First General Elections, on the basis of the popular votes, had been a minimal winning coalition.[53] This pattern continued in subsequent General Elections too through the working of the "multiplier principle" arising out of the division of the opposition votes, until it failed to get a majority of parliamentary seats in the 1977, 1989 and subsequent General Elections thereafter.

It is not only the Congress Party which is having an intra-party coalition but also other parties like the Janata Party and the Communist Party. According to Madhu Dandavate: "The Janata Party was apparently a single party, but in reality it was a combination of the Socialist

Party, Bharatiya Jan Sangh, Congress (O), BLD, and other group dissident Congressmen led by Jagjivan Ram and H.N. Bahuguna".[54] The Congress for Democracy (CFD) of Jagjivan Ram, of course, merged with the Janata Party after the General Elections.[55] The Janata Government itself was a coalition with its allies consisting of heterogeneous elements. The point sought to be raised in this section is that the Janata Party like the Congress Party had an intra-party coalition because of the structure and nature of its composition.

Much earlier, in 1964, the Indian Communist Party also indicated that there was an intra-party coalition when it broke into two parts, the Communist Party of India and the Communist Party of India (Marxist). While both of them ideologically belong to the left the former is tilting towards the centre while the latter swings into the extreme left. There are many other splinter groups of the Indian Communist Party ranging from the Marxist-Leninist brand to the revolutionary groups. All these developments in the Communist Camp show that there exists an intra-party coalition in the party which ultimately paves the way to disunity in the party. Of course, in recent years there is an attempt to bring the CPI and CP(M) together in that the former has started a unity move with the latter. It is yet to be seen how far this policy of reapproachment can work out in the near future among the communists particularly when there are ideological differences among them.[56]

This kind of an exercise in political futurology has also been made in 1984 through a symposium on the issue of *A Coalition Future* in the July issue of the *Seminar.* While stating presumably on the problem of inter-party coalition the symposium refers to "the old consensus culture of the Indian National Congress",[57] and added that: "Actually, coalition politics merely reflect the earlier consensus-making politics of the Indian National Congress, but in a more institutionalised form".[58] The key word here is on the institutionalisation of coalition, intra-party or otherwise. In the past, there was practically no institutionalisation of coalition as such. Today, however, it has become more increasingly necessary to have such an institutionalisation if we are interested in a stable coalition. Indeed Harold Wilson, the former Prime Minister of the United Kingdom had pointed out to the possibility of an institutionalised inter-party coalition. He said: "In any case, every party leader who forms a party-based government is the head of a coalition. Every major party is itself a coalition".[59]

The problem in India is that we have yet to institutionalise an intra-party coalition and not to speak about the inter-party coalition. At the inter-party coalition we used to hear about the Common Needs Programme, the National Agenda and the like. But where is the head of the coalition excepting the Steering Committee where there are so many heads. The situation is much worse in the case of an inter-party coalition where the regional satraps are gaining more power due to regionalisation of politics and the head of the party organisation at the national level has all the time to keep tapping on the possible toppling game by these regional satraps. Ash Narain Roy has aptly remarked in his "Stress on Consensus" in the governance of our country that: "Surprisingly in India, it is the intra-party and not so much inter-party divisions that have rocked the coalition governments."[60]

SECTION 4: INTER-PARTY COALITION

Starting from the Interim Government of 1946, the pattern of governance in India was basically coalitional in nature. There were the Socialists like Nehru, Conservatives like Patel, Scheduled Castes like Ambedkar, minorities like Maulana Abul Kalam Azad and Baldev Singh. Most of them, no doubt belonged to the Indian National Congress. But the Interim Government was not entirely under the Congress. A sort of a coalition representing different shades of opinion in the country was tried in order to include the proper political representation of able leaders from all sections of the Indian society. Shanmukham Chetty was another Cabinet Minister who did not belong to the Congress Party. Some others like

John Mathai, C.H. Bhaba, Gopalaswamy Ayangar and C.D. Deshmukh did not belong to any political party. They "were brought into the Cabinet because of their ability and experience in other fields".[61] Or as late as 1980 Hazrat Abdul Shah Bukhari a strong critic of the Congress during the 1977 Elections became a supporter of the Congress during the 1977 Elections became a supporter of the Congress Party in the 1980 Elections.[62]

There was a historical background leading to such an arrangement. In the beginning, the Congress movement itself was composed of the Communist Party, the Hindu Mahasabha, and the Socialist Party.[63] Later on, they pushed out of the Congress and at times some of them came back to it. But right from the First General Elections of 1952, the Congress as a political party which had liberated India from foreign rule could not secure a majority in the States of Madras, Orissa, Patiala and East Punjab States Union, and Travancore-Cochin. The Congress, however, could manage to avoid non Congress Governments in these states barring for sometimes in PEPSU. Mohit Sen observes that: In fact coalitions began with the First General Elections in 1952 itself. In the Madras Presidency, a broad non Congress United Front with T. Prakasam as the leader and undivided CPI as the main component won a majority in the Assembly Elections".[64] However, "C. Rajagopalachari on the instruction of Pt. Nehru was sent to break up the united front and restore the Congress monopoly of power".[65]

A similar account was given by E.M.S. Namboodripad that in each of the States of Travancore-Cochin, Madras, and PEPSU there was a United Front of parties which jointly fought the elections. They had even secured an absolute majority of seats. But the United Fronts in Travancore-Cochin and Madras were prevented from forming coalition Governments because the Congress using the Heads of States and through defections could form the governments. Only in PEPSU the United Front of parties was allowed to form a non-Congress coalition government but fell after a few months.[66] Thus, PEPSU had the distinction of being the first State in the Indian

Union, after independence, to form a non-Congress government with the inter-party coalition.

The Congress Party was not at all happy to have allowed the non-Congress coalition to come into existence. If any coalition government has to be formed the Congress should have been one of the parties. That was why after the PEPSU non-Congress coalition fell from power, the Congress could form a minority government with the support of other parties but had to go for a fresh poll in 1954. The same was the case in Andhra Pradesh when the Congress had to go for a fresh poll in 1955. Only in Travancore-Cochin the Congress had to accept a minority government formed by the Praja Socialist Party ostensibly with the support of the Congress.[67] In Orissa, the Congress entered into a coalition government with the Ganatantra Party from 1957 to 1961; and in Kerala with the PSP and the Muslim League in 1960.[68] In the 1962 Elections, the Congress could form the governments in Rajasthan (88 out of 176 seats), Madhya Pradesh (142 out of 288 seats) with the support of independents.[69]

Similarly, the non-Congress parties over since 1962 had entered into coalitions among themselves as well as with some Congress defectors. Some of these coalitions were called United Fronts. But Kothari has rightly questioned whether such types of coalition are really "coalitionable".[70] Its nomenclature of anti-Congress United Fronts coalitions, however, varies from State to State. In some States they were called Left Fronts. In this connection, it has been observed by Kothari that these non-Congress multi-party coalitions differ from their Western counterparts. This difference arises mainly due to the fact that in India, unlike in the West, there has been a constant "shifting support structure" in the constituencies and "a legislative patch work resulting from it."[71]

Sometimes the same party, like the Congress, splits into two parts. Either the dominant party like one led by Indira Gandhi or the subordinate one led by the traditional leaders of the party called the organisational Congress were always seeking allies from among the non-

Congress parties. This situation often leads to the emergence of "rival coalitions".[72] For example, after the Congress split in 1969, while the Congress (O) was seeking allies to topple the Congress (I) government, the latter had managed to form a majority government with the outside support of the Dravidra Munnetra Kazakham and the C.P.I.[73]

In view of the changing political situation in the country, both the Congress and non-Congress parties have to adjust themselves with the changing times by entering into coalitions of one form or another whichever suits them at a particular period of time. After the 1977 Elections the Morarji's ministry was "a coalition of several parties" though he assumed office as "a leader of a single party".[74] But the Janata coalition came to power only to be replaced by the Choudhury Charan Singh's coalition government with the support of the Congress (I) in 1979. However, within a few months that coalition government also fell from power.[75]

The Congress played the same role after the 1989 Elections. After the Election, the National Front coalition government was formed by V.P. Singh with the outside support of the newly constituted party of the Bharatiya Janata Party out of the earlier Jana Sangh. But after eleven months in power, the BJP withdrew its support. This paved the way for another coalition government headed by Chandrashekhar with the support of the Congress (I) from outside. This government also fell within a couple of months with the resignation of Chandrashekhar.[76] The resignation of Chandrashekhar was essentially due to the plan of the Congress Party in the game of coalition-making and coalition-breaking.

After the fall of the Janata coalition government we have witnessed other inter-party coalitions. The Janata Party and the allies formed the United Democratic Front; and the BJP and the Lok Dal formed the National Democratic Alliance. Perhaps the Lok Dal or the Janata (Secular) had realised that there was nothing wrong in forging an alliance on coalition with the BJP which was secular as per its constitution.[77]

The other examples of groupings of parties for forming a coalition can be found in the States including those in North-East India. Sometimes, it is rather strange to find parties with different ideologies had to form a coalition for the purpose of Government formation. After the 1967 Elections in Bihar, "disparate" parties like the CPI, Jana Sangh with the support from outside of the CPI (M) and Swatantra Party came together for the purpose of coalition government making.[78] Or in West Bengal there were 14 political parties in the first coalition. Then in the next government with the Leftists and the splintered Congress joined hands in a coalition government, in 1969, which according to its leader Ajoy Mukherjee there was "No civilized government in West Bengal" and started launching "a civil resistance movement against his own government and went on a fast".[79] The case of inter-party coalitions in North-East India will be dealt with separately.

A word about the inter-party coalitions among the Communists would be in order. In the beginning the Communists would like to base their coalition politics on "electoral considerations". But the "electoral front" is not the role arena of struggle. It is not a means "to attain power in the States or at the Centre", but "to strengthen the unity of the people".[80] For example, the CPI (M) in its Party Programme adopted in 1964 pledged itself to "unite with all the patriotic forces of the nation, i.e., those who are interested in sweeping away all the remnants of pre-capitalist society; in carrying out the agrarian revolution in a thorough manner and in the interests of the peasantry; in eliminating all traces of foreign capital; and in removing all obstacles in the path of radical culture."[81] In other words, the need for inter-party coalition among the Leftists is not only for an electoral front before the elections nor a United Front coalition after the election but also to develop "other forms of parliamentary and extra-parliamentary struggles to mobilise the people around the programme of Left and democratic Front."[82]

Namboodripad has succintly summed up the inter party coalitions among the Left and democratic forces in these words: "The politics of coalition or United Front which our party has worked out is therefore different from that of several other parties, ruling and opposition, which are interested in coalitions with the sole intention of winning such electoral victories as enable them either to remain in power or secure it through parliamentary maneuvers. Ours is in fact a coalition of political forces with the objective of changing the correlation of national and international forces, electoral struggle being the means to obtain this objective."[83]

An attempt has been made in this section to find out the attitudes of the Congress, non-Congress and Communist parties to the issue of inter-party coalitions in India. Till 1952, inter-party coalitions, by and large, had been based on the consideration for the good of the country, society and its people. The main consideration was on the merits of political leaders irrespective of party affiliations. Even if political ideologies were sometimes in conflict with one another these were sorted out and the same had been mutually resolved. There was then no rigid categorisation between a centrist, a leftist or a rightist. It was only after the 1952 Elections that the non-Congress and Communist parties had become anti-Congress and the Congress in turn would like to monopolise political power. But it was not that easy for both the groups.

By 1969 it was amply clear that an inter-party coalition was quite necessary if the political parties were to survive. While continuing to play the game of power struggle, political parties have, of late, realised that the era of coalition, whether one likes it or not, has come to stay. Even the BJP, once an untouchable, has become respectable as its party Constitution is secular and not communal. What remains to be done as in the case of intra-party coalition is the institutionalistion of inter-party coalition. The institutionalisation of inter-party coalition does require the review of the Anti-Defection Law under the Tenth Schedule to the Constitution of India. it is our considered opinion that in view of the fact that inter-party coalition is a necessity we have to make it a stable one. To ensure the stability of inter-party coalition the Tenth Schedule has to be suitably amended so as to make rooms for the institutionalisation of coalition politics both at the national and the State Levels.

SECTION 5: THEORIES OF COALITION

Here, we propose to discuss the two main theories of coalition: (a) maximisation theory of winning coalitions of the Zero-sum games of William H. Riker; and (b) policy-based winning coalitions of Abram de Swaan along with the policy-based theories of coalition formation and coalition behaviour of Robert Axelrod.[84] The first theory is associated with decision-making theories as already mentioned in Section 2 above; and the second theory with the theory of consociational democracy of grand proportional autonomy and mutual veto coalitions of Arend Lijphart.

William H. Riker in his *Theory of Political Coalitions* (1962) based his study of coalitions more on the political theory of behaviour rather than on the study of political behaviour itself, particularly on the mathematical theory of games.[85] In this theory he is greatly influenced by the writings of economists like John Von Neuman and Oskar Morgenstern's *The Theory of Games and Economic Behaviour* (1944). While agreeing with the economists on the model of Zero-sum games in economics, he pointed out that in politics and war it is the model of non-zero-sum games which predominates.[86] The Zero-sum games theory follows the minimax theorem where one side gains and the other side loses in the economic games for authoritative allocation of resources.[87] But in the political non-Zero-sum games for authoritative allocation of values, like power, the maximisation of power theorem with the help of a coalition sometimes makes the gainers to become the losers.[88] However, there are exceptions in the case of the Indian National Congress immediately after independence, when it perceived itself in a Zero-sum game fashion.[89]

Apart from the Zero-sum and the non-zero-sum games, Riker also refers to "n-person-sum game" when side-payments are a consideration for joining a coalition.[90] Further, any such coalition may be described as a "winning", "losing", "blocking", or "grand" coalition.[91] While winning and losing coalitions have been referred to above, the grand coalition or a coalition of the whole is examplified by Riker in the form of the Indian National Congress in 1947-48.[92] The blocking coalition, on the other hand, refers to a position when no further moves are possible in coalition-making. This usually happens when the unattached members are absorbed into two coalitions.[93] When a coalition is neither winning, losing or blocking, it is no coalition at all. At most, it may be simply called a "protocoalition" in which a member merely moves within a sub-set of decision-making where he has no weight nor can impose his will on the main decision-making body.[94] It is in such a situation that unlike the dynamic model of coalition-making, a position of a static model of coalition-making has been reached.[95]

From the discussions of the theories of political coalitions, Riker is firmly of the view that a general theory has greater advantage over adhoc or "inductive" theories.[96] In his n-person games theory which falls under the category of a general theory he develops the three propositions of the size principle, the strategic principle, and the disequilibrium principle.[97] The size principle refers to the winning coalitions which tend toward the minimal winning size. In the strategic principle it is the assertion that "in systems or bodies in which the size principle is operative, participants in the final stages of coalition-formation should and do more toward a minimum winning coalition".[98] It is the disequilibrium principle which combines the first two principles of size and strategy. The disequilibrium principle is the assertion that when the size and strategic principles are unstable it leads toward "the elimination of participants" arising out of decisions without regard to stakes.[99]

After discussing the three main principles of political coalitions Riker refers to the study of politics, in the words of Aristotle as "a practical science" in the sense that people study it not only to discover reality but also to manipulate it.[100] The problem of manipulation is not so much in a two-person-sum game relating to the authoritative allocation of resources as in economics which follows the minimax theorem but in the n-person-sum game relating to the authoritative allocation of values in politics. In the latter game, while trying to research the equilibrium point the standard of "good" and "rational" play may not be reached through the art of manipulation. The reality is that n-person games as in politics are concerned with coalitions directly rather than strategies. Indeed as Riker observes: "The absolute end product of coalition-formation is, however, a two-person game"[101] where political reality outweighs the political manipulation.

But whether the games theory is a Zero-sum or non-zero-sum, a two-person or n-person game has some correlation with the second theory mentioned in this lecture on the policy-based winning coalition theory of Abram de Swaan in his *Coalition Theories and Cabinet Formations* (1973). His theory is based on power maximisation through pay-offs as well as through ideological and policy affinities but with minimum winning coalition.[102] While discussing this theory, a reference may also be made to the concept of consociational democracy of grand, proportional, autonomy, and mutual veto coalitions of Arend Lijphart. Here, it may be mentioned that though the theory of coalitions "to serve as a theory of politics has not yet been developed",[103] we cannot avoid discussing part of political theory in trying to understand the theory of coalitions. Lijphart, while taking into consideration the political aspect of coalition is of the opinion that since democracy, as a concept, can not be explicitly defined, the term "polyarchy" used by Robert A. Dahl may perhaps be applied for the democratic system in a pluralistic society.[104] Polyarchy is not a system of government which may contain all democratic ideals but it only approximates them to a reasonable degree.[105] Further, in a plural society, a society is divided into what Harry Eckstein calls "segmental cleavages".[106] These cleavages may be based on religious, ideological, linguistics, regional, social or ethnic nature.[107]

With this observation, Lijphart comes to the question of his concept of consociational democracy in relation to the policy-based winning coalition theory. According to him, consociational government consists of four characteristics:

(a) In a parliamentary system consociational democracy can be defined as a government by a grand coalition of all the significant political segments of the plural society;
(b) In such a Government there is what is called a mutual veto or "concurrent majority" rule which protects the minority interests as well;
(c) The grand coalition government provides a proportionality of political representation, appointment of civil services, and allocation of public funds; and
(d) It also provides a high degree of autonomy for each segment in running its own internal affairs.[108]

If we apply the above four characteristics, we may say that the practice of coalition politics in the Indian parliamentary system has more or less included the first three characteristics. But so far as the fourth characteristic is concerned, till the time of writing, it does not appear to have been achieved in the Indian political scene. The experiments under the V.P. Singh's National Front, and the H.D. Deve Gowda and I.K. Gujral's United Front coalition governments are quite illustrative. The lack of internal autonomy of the various segments of the coalition government is one of the reasons for the short tenures of these coalition governments which would not be fully consociational in form and content.

The central features of consociational governments would, therefore, include a "segmented pluralism" broadened by "segmental cleavages" in a plural society and combined with "concordant democracy" [109] The term segmental cleavage has already been discussed above. So far as segmented pluralism, it refers to segmental cleavages of a religious and ideological nature accompanied by political co-operation. Concordant democracy, on the other hand, refers to a strategy of conflict management by co-operation and agreement among the leaders of different segments instead of conflict management by competition and majority decision.[110] Here again, India does not seem to have the above features in its experiments on coalition politics. The segmental cleavages of a religious and ideological nature in the Janata coalition government was not accompanied by political cooperation. Similarly, all the coalition governments at the national level have followed the strategy of conflict management by competition and majority decision rather than by co-operation and agreement.

While commenting on the Indian experience, it does not mean that India does not fit in with the concept of the grand coalition of consociational democracy. It is only that a grand coalition is "inherently oversized". The fact is that Lijphart while pointing out to the disadvantages of consociational government, among other things, he said that such a government is more successful in smaller countries because of direct and indirect effects. That is, the elites in smaller countries directly know each other personally and indirectly the system is less complex in governance.[111] Whatever may be the size of countries, the most important method of consociational government of a grand coalition either of a two-person zero-sum or n-person zero-sum game is implemented through mutual veto, proportionality and segmental autonomy.[112]

The form or typology of a coalition government of a policy-based winning coalition theory may be either consociational or adversarial, coalescent or competitive, which corresponds to Gabriel Almond's typology of centrifugal and centripetal types.[113] The following diagrams may illustrate the point:

Structure of Society

Elite Behaviour	Homogenous	Plural
Coalescent	Depoliticised Democracy	Consociational Democracy
Adversarial	Centripetal Democracy	Centrifugal Democracy

Thus, in a plural society like India, the elite behaviour tends to be adversarial rather than coalescent. That is, centrifugal democracy is more pronounced than consociational democracy. This is one of the reasons why we have yet to have a stable coalition politics in the country. Lijphart has cautioned that: "For many of the plural societies of the non-Western world, therefore, the realistic choice is not between the British model of democracy and the consociational democracy but between consociational democracy and no democracy at all."[114] "It is also assumed" he said, "that the consociational and British models are the ideal-type alternatives and that there is no as yet undiscovered third alternative".[115] The comparative success of coalition politics in these two models may be graphically illustrated thus:[116]

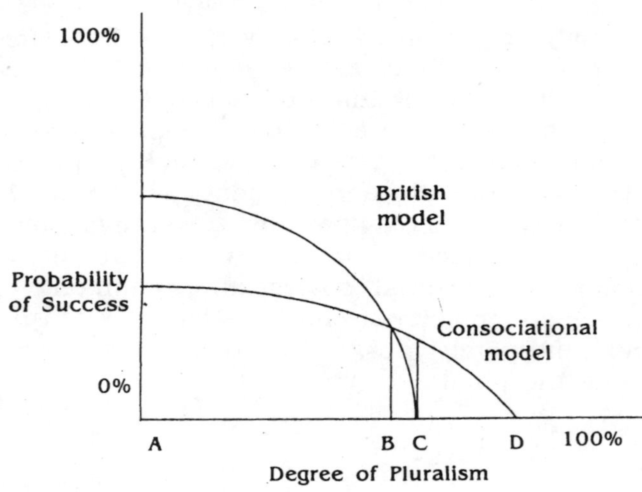

The success of consociational model again depends on which kind of coalition a political society fits in. There are generally four principles which we have already described above. In summing up, we may again refer to these principles of a grand coalition, a proportional coalition, an autonomy coalition, and a mutual veto coalition.[117] In case India finds that the British model is no longer applicable and opts for a consociational model, it may either adopt any or a combination of the above four principles of coalition.

So far we have discussed only the two main theories of coalition in the context of parliamentary system of government and politics. These two theories are more or less applicable in the Indian political situation. That is why we have not made any attempt to find out the other theories of coalition pertaining to other political systems prevailing in other parts of the world. The political experiences in single party communist or non-communist countries or governments run by military leaders may, of course, require a different set of theories of coalition. The theories of coalition in the presidential system of government and politics also have not been explored in this lecture. However, we firmly believe that some of the basic tenets of the above theories may be appropriately applicable in the other political systems as well. For the purpose of North-East Indian government and politics, we have assumed that both the games theory and the policy-based theory of coalitions are in operation either separately or in a combination of the two, depending on the political circumstances prevailing in the particular political unit of the region. The theoretical aspect of coalition in North-East India will be further discussed and highlighted along with the study of coalition politics in the region in the two subsequent lectures below.

SECTION 6: PATTERNS OF COALITION

Iqbal Narain and Mohan Lal in their "Coalitional Politics, National Building and Administration: From Myths to Reality"[118] while referring to Rajni Kothari's work on the intra-Congress party coalition-making in our country express that their work would be on inter-party coalitional politics in India rather than on intra-party coalition.[119] The various aspects of intra-party and inter-party coalition have already been discussed in Section 4 above. Here we propose to give a brief outline of the several patterns of coalition politics from the writings of Narain and Lal.

The first pattern refers to an electoral alliance-turned governmental coalition. This has been the pattern that we witness in the case of State Elections ever since 1967. In this pattern there is a pre-poll alliance which alliance when achieving a majority formed itself into a coalition government. The cases of Kerala in 1967 and 1970; Orissa in 1967, Punjab in 1970; and West Bengal in 1969 elections may be cited as examples of such a pattern of electoral alliances turned government coalitions.[120]

The other pattern is the one in which there is no pre-poll alliance, but after the elections, there is an arrangement among the different counterparts to forge ahead for forming a coalition government. This happened after the Fourth General Elections in Bihar, Madhya Pradesh and Uttar Pradesh.[121]

The third pattern of coalition is the case of an ideologically homogeneous governmental coalition like the Janata Congress-Swatantra coalition in Orissa.[122]

The next pattern unlike the ideologically homogenous coalition is the kind of coalition with the ideologically heterogeneous elements as in the case of Samyukta Vidhayak Dal governments in Bihar, Madhya Pradesh and Uttar Pradesh.[123]

Fifthly, there is the coalition as among the Leftists of West Bengal.[124] The United Front of West Bengal with pre-poll arrangements and the formation of a coalition government has been experimenting with coalitional politics quite successfully for almost three decades now.

As compared to the Leftists, we also have coalition politics among the Rightists. Orissa and Punjab have given us the examples of such coalitions in the forms of the Janata Congress-Swatantra coalition in Orissa and the Akali Dal-Jan Sangh coalition in Punjab.[125]

The last of the patterns given by Narain and Lal is the coalition between the Leftists and the Rightists which is called the Centrist governmental coalition. Such a coalition may be found in Uttar Pradesh where at one time the Congress (O) and the Congress (R) joined hands together in forming the government or at another time between the Bharatiya Kranti Dal and the Congress (R).[126]

The list of patterns of coalition is in fact not exhaustive. The contributors themselves have admitted that: "we are still travelling on the road to coalition making and there are several patterns of coalitional politics in the country."[127] Indeed, there is "need of empirical enquiry into the dynamics of coalitional politics to replace normative myths with realistic formulations in regard to the efficacy of coalitional experiments in India."[128]

That is one reason why some other writers like Mahendra Prasad talks of levels of coalition-building instead of patterns of coalition.[129] According to Prasad there are four such levels in which some of these levels of coalition overlap with the patterns of coalition discussed above. The first level of coalition is called the "Electoral Coalition" in which "a Front" is "formed prior to the election" as in the case of the Janata Coalition and the National Front Coalition.[130] The second level of coalition is the "Legislative Coalition" which is "a Front between two sets of parties, one forming the government (by one or more parties), and the other extending legislative support to it without joining the Cabinet," like the United Front Government at the Centre and the early part of the P.V. Narasimha Rao government.[131]

Thirdly, there is the "Executive Coalition" when a group of parties formed a coalition government like the Janata government or the United Front government at the Centre.[132] The fourth and the last level of coalition-building is the "Federal Coalition" when the same political parties are simultaneously forming a coalition both at the national and State levels as during the Janata regime.[133] Thus, in this classification, there is a subtle difference between the Executive and Legislative coalitions. As Kaare Strom commented: "Minority governments violate the expectation that executive and legislative coalitions are identical."[134]

Unlike Narain and Lal, and Prasad, who write about patterns and levels of coalitions, O.P. Minocha discusses about the type of coalitions which are similar to levels of coalitions.[135] According to him there are three types or levels of coalitions-parliamentary, electoral and governmental. A parliamentary coalition takes place when there is a minority government supported by different political parties or with an arrangement with these parties for support from outside. It may also happen that a minority government survives because of the tactical reasons adopted by opposition parties. Sometimes, such a minority government is also known as a government by "jumping majorities".[136] Whatever may be the name either a minority government or a government by jumping majorities such a government falls under the category of a parliamentary coalition.

The electoral coalition of Minocha is the pre-poll alliance or a coalition in which two or more parties have mutual co-operation during the electoral battle. It may take the form of not setting up candidates excepting the party having a chance to win. There may also be mutual withdrawal of candidates from different constituencies to avoid splitting of votes. This type of coalition is known as an electoral coalition.

In the governmental coalition other types or sub-types of coalitions may be noted. There is governmental coalition in the form of a National Government where most, if not all, of the parties join together to meet a national emergency arising out of war or economic crisis. This type of coalition does not generally take place during peace time conditions. The other type of governmental coalition which may be called a "responsive coalition" is the fusion of political parties in the government arising out of contemporary national issues. We have yet to have a perfect example of such a coalition. The Janata

Government is the nearest example of this type of coalition.[137]

The common type of governmental coalition in India is the "power-sharing coalition" where two or more political parties who can not each gain a majority combine to form a majority government. The National Front Government, the United Front Government, and the present BJP-led coalition government at the Centre are examples of power-sharing coalition who continue to compete electorally with coalition partners while they are in the same government.[138]

Thus, in post-independence India, excepting the coalition in the form of a National Government, we have the examples of almost every other pattern, level or type of coalition discussed above or in the words of Blackwell, "kinds of coalition governments" whether at the national or State levels. During the post Twelfth General Elections to the Indian Lok Sabha in 1998 there were indications that a national government may be formed in view of the fact that none of the major national parties could form a government on its own. There were doubts also that any coalition government, be it the BJP-led, Congress-led or United Front-led coalition government would be able to provide a stable government. However, the idea of a national coalition government does not seem to be acceptable to the political parties during the period of peaceful conditions in the country.

In the foregoing paragraphs we have discussed about the various patterns, levels, types and kinds of coalition politics and governments. We have also cited examples from the Indian experience both at the national and State levels. But we have yet to have a more detailed literature on the coalition politics and governments in North-East India. While discussing about the coalition politics and governments in North-East India in the Second and Third Lectures in this series, we propose to simultaneously analyse the processes of coalition-making and coalition-breaking in the region bearing in mind the above patterns, levels and types of coalitions. But it is very significant to note at this juncture that while we may give any of the above labels to any coalition in North-East India, the fact remains that by and large, coalitions in North-East India during the British period were quite different from the coalitions in the post-independence period. We shall give a more detailed discussion when we pass on to the respective Lectures on coalition politics in North-East India.

SECTION 7: SUMMING UP

After discussing the various aspects of coalition politics, Nikhil Chakravarty, comments that in the case of India, "there is not a ghost of a chance to go in for one party rule. Coalition politics has just become inescapable".[139] It is also very interesting to note the observations made by Rajni Kothari on the 1998 Lok Sabha Elections. In his "Messages in Ballots" he says that: "The era of coalitions had arrived but the parties and the groups that were coalescing were unable to provide a credible and stable framework of governance".[140] More than that there has been a change in the coalition politics at the national level due to the fact that: "There had taken place a growing regionalization of politics".[141]

This regionalisation of politics brings about a change in the coalition politics of India. As Kothari has rightly remarked: "The coalitional model was still operating but now as a more moderating force than before, one in which large national parties were being forced to accept the need for alliances and accommodations with a variety of both old and new parties and individuals. And above all with regional parties whom they were earlier prone to brush aside".[142] According to him, the net result of the 1998 Lok Sabha Elections "was that whereas national politics was moving toward a coalitional model, at the State level it was moving away from it and towards some kind of a two party model" excepting the States of Bihar and Uttar Pradesh.[143] Thus, the present Indian coalition framework has forced both "the Hindutva framework of BJP" and "the dynastic framework of the Congress" towards moderate position because of the new political compulsions of carrying various allies with them. This moderating force also keeps "the Congress from total collapse" and "the BJP from its earlier extremist stance".[144]

The question now is whether the coalition framework in the context of Indian politics is good or bad for the country. It is indeed a very difficult question with no definite answer to it. At one extreme, there is always "the pride about majority governments" and at the other extreme, "the prejudice against coalitional politics".[145] The balanced view, however, seems to have been the argument that, "it should not be taken for granted that, coalitional governments, whatever their type and stage of growth, are *per se* dysfunctional to nation-building and effective administration, all the more because we are still travelling on the way to coalition making and there are several patterns of coalitional politics in the country".[146] Hence, the question is not that "coalitional governments are superior to majority governments or vice-versa".[147] What is to be done instead is to have an "empirical enquiry into the dynamics of coalitional politics to replace normative myths with realistic formulations in regard to the efficiency of coalitional experiments in India".[148] Till then we should not come to any conclusion whether coalitional politics is good or bad, and that "coalitional politics and political development go ill together" [149]

The problem faced by coalition politics and governments in India is mainly on the issue of their stability. The observations made by A.R. Desai in 1975 are still relevant today. He says that: "with the prospect of coalition ministries . . . the bourgeois parliamentary government will confront an epoch of tremendous instability".[150] The second issue raised by Desai is on the efficacy of the common minimum programmes of coalition ministries. Today, apart from the common minimum programmes, coalition partners are also talking about the national agenda. Whatever the term used by coalition partners, the fact remains that they continue to get the members involved in competitive politics.

Such being the present political situation it is very difficult to expect the parties to bring about a stable coalition on the basis of mere common minimum programmes on national agenda. That is why Desai raises his doubts on the effectiveness of such attempts. He also goes on to say that: "Efforts are being made to discover whether a stable democratic government based on a common programme of political action and founded on principled alliances of parties with similar perspectives and programmes could evolve or not."[151] Our Indian experience tells us that we still keep our finger crossed when it comes to the question of stability of a coalition politics or government in the country.

Assuming that we have a sound common minimum programme or national agenda it is not guaranteed that we would have successful governments. It all depends on the nature and character of each coalition. We may not be able to generalise that each and every coalition would be successful. Even a one-party government sometimes proves to be a failure due to intra-party coalition. And the rate of failures in inter-party coalition would be much more as borne out by experiences in our country and elsewhere. This is perhaps due to the fact that the one-party government like the Congress Party has been regarded as the "Great Tradition" while the non-Congress coalitions are regarded as "LIttle Traditions".[152] Besides these two traditions have also followed two different theories in explaining the relationship between society and polity. The Great traditions tend to follow the "Instrumentalist" theory of the Centrists and the Leftists while the Little Traditions are Rightists in nature and follow the "primordialist" theory.[153]

J.S. Bali in his "The New Coalition Experiment: India Metamorphosis"[154] has referred to the examples of such failures in France and Italy. He cited the findings of Geffory Sack, the Washington economist, on the experience of coalition governments. According to Sack, "a coalition of two or three parties on a fixed agreed programme has been a resounding success in Germany and to a certain extent in France" [155] The rate of failures are very high where a coalition is formed by "more than six or seven parties" and such a coalition "has led to instability, lack of economic progress, etc".[156] Because of the existence of innumerable parties in the French and Italian coalitions there have been many coalition governments within a short span of time. For example, Italy has seen 55 coalition governments in 50 years and in France the average life span of coalition governments would be about nine months.[157] Desai has very neatly summed up about the success of any coalition government when he says: "The success of the coalition governments depends upon the nature and character of parties, which form alliances for forming such governments.[158]

In India too we have had many coalitions both at the Centre and in the States. At the national level there are twelve coalitions ever since independence including the Interim Government; one one-party majority coalition (Janata); four one-party minority coalitions (Indira Gandhi's government during the Congress split as well as in the latter part of the government, P.V. Narasimha Rao's government during the early part, and the BJP 13-day coalition); six multi-party minority coalitions (three National Fronts, two United Fronts and the BJP—led coalition of 18 parties). Here, it is not possible to give the whole list of coalitions in the States as there are too many of them. All the same, when one examines the tenure of these coalitions, the longest would be about 2½ years as in the case of the Janata coalition. In most cases they are less than a year. Mahendra Prasad while studying the tenure of these coalitions refers to what has been opined in Blackwell's *Encyclopaedia of Political Institutions* (1987) that: "Recent studies have shown considerable variation in durability between different kinds of coalition governments. Minimal winning coalitions exhibit substantially greater stability than minority coalitions and oversized governments, and can prove as stable as single party governments".[159]

Whether the coalition is good or bad, stable or unstable, there is definitely a certain amount of stress and strain in a coalition government compared to a one-party government. To reduce such stresses and strains it is incumbent upon the coalition partners to make necessary adjustments and compromises. The leading article on "Coalition Politics under Strain" has rightly pointed out that "coalition politics and the running of a coalition government require delicate adjustments and compromises".[160]

These adjustments and compromises are usually in the form of mutual co-operation if the coalition is to become successful. Riker has already hinted that such "Co-operation will benefit the players".[161] In case such co-operation is not forth-coming the game is called "inessential" in which the players are still trying "to form coalitions and act through these in order to secure their advantage".[162] The inessential game suggests that there are different patterns, levels, types, or kinds of coalitions. "Different coalitions", says Riker "may have different strength".[163] But the only successful coalition is a winning coalition. The prescription for such a coalition is that: "A winning coalition will have to divide its proceeds among its members, and each member must be satisfied with the division in order that a stable solution obtains".[164]

In the Indian context we do also need such a winning coalition through co-operation, adjustments and compromises. Our political analysts have fully grasped about the need for a stable and successful coalition in view of the fact that we can no longer avoid the era of coalition. Balraj Mehta in his "Coalition Politics: Meaningful and Responsive" has commented that: "The conflict of interest in the economy and society, can not be contained under a flimsy political-power sharing arrangement . . . It is time for political alignment to the policy rather than personality based. This is the only basis for coalition politics to become meaningful and responsive to the will and aspiration of the people".[165] Another leading article on "Party Alignment Sans Ideology" also expresses the same sentiment when it says: "The need is for a coalition of parties committed to pro-people socio-economic development and preservation and strengthening of the sovereign status of India in the World Order".[166]

At the same time there are indications already about the alarming political situation in the country when coalition governments can not run the governance of the nation and the States. But inspite of this pessimistic outlook on the present political instability in the country there are also optimistic options about the stability of coalition governments in the absence of an alternative one-party government. Writing on "Coalition Governments: Perspective from Culture History", S.C. Malik has pointed out that throughout our Indian civilisation we have the experiences of successful coalitions. He says that "the formation of explicit governments either at the Centre or in the States seems to indicate instability. Similar alarmist opinions are expressed when coalition governments were formed in the States from 1967 onwards. But have we thought that perhaps we ought to give this system a chance since it may well suit over socio-cultural system? A true final policy for the Indian civilization is this".[167]

Malik further contends that the current political situation is in fact following the pattern of political behaviour that we have inherited from our own history. He confirms his observation by referring to historical events taking place in our country. He says: "different groups have learnt to reconcile and coalesce its functional groups or form associations . . . . Historically, alliances and counter-alliances at the political level, based on multi-caste or multi-group associations have also been a common feature. These have been formed successfully through the skill of negotiations . . . . Co-existence, the middle path, moderation, consensus and coalition have been the behavioural patterns".[168]

All the above summary is only to indicate that whether one likes it or not we have to contend ourselves with the present era of coalition in India. What is needed is only the institutionalisation of coalition as among some European nations. The present writer in his "Party Government is a vital principle of a Representative Government" has opined that: "It is now quite clear that in the case of India both national fragmentation and regionalism have brought about an era of coalitional politics at the Centre and in some States. But . . . this regionalisation of national level politics with its coalitional politics may not at all bring about political stability as among many European countries".[169] He further states that: "In European countries, their cultural systems provide proportional representation and thereby institutionalised coalitional politics. Such kind of coalitional politics are quite stable because there are stable regional political parties with distinct social bases and clear stable political programmes. There is a clear division of Right and Left programmes and ideology from which a clear choice can be made".[170]

The role of bureaucracy in coalition government and politics has also been highlighted. Comparing the Indian experience with the European practices he is of the view that: "This is not so in the present context in our country. Coalitional politics here is in a fluid state as yet. In addition, the bureaucracy in European democracies have been to further cement the administrative foundation and thereby strengthening the stability of governmental programmes in a coalitional government as in France and Italy. But in India, in the changing political scenario, the bureaucracy has yet to be tested and may instead be another source of political instability due to regional influences and loyalties".[171] Hence, while commuting oı the 1996 Lok Sabha Elections he is of the opinion that: "Coalitional politics in India after 1996 elections based mainly on regionalism may not, therefore, be a mechanism for bringing order and stability at least in the near future".[172]

Today after witnessing the 1998 Lok Sabha Elections and some State Assembly Elections the present writer has not changed his view. He is convinced that perhaps we have learnt very little from our experiments with coalition politics in the country. Whatever knowledge our political leaders have gained through coalition politics is mainly for coalition-making and coalition-breaking. We have yet to gain the knowledge of coalition-management for the purpose of a sustainable and stable coalition. Perhaps Alfred Tennyson in his poem "Locksley Hall" (1837–38) in a different context had already forseen our present political conditions. He writes: "Knowledge comes, but wisdom lingers, and I linger on the shore, And the individual withers, and the world is more and more".[173]

North-East India is no exception to the points raised in the above summary. The region has been experiencing coalition politics and governments for a very long time. It is not merely the product of post-independence era nor of the post-1967 State or regional coalitions in the country. Historically, coalition-making and coalition-breaking has been the usual behavioural pattern of the various communities of North East India both in war and politics. In the following two Lectures while bearing in mind the above theoretical considerations, we propose to discuss about coalition politics in North-East India. The Second Lecture will pay a special attention to coalition politics in the region during the British period. When we use the term North East India during that period we refer essentially to coalition politics in Assam which covered all the territories of the existing States barring the Native States of Khasi Hills, Manipur and Tripura; and the Frontier Tracts, and Controlled and Unadministered Areas. In the Third Lecture, we will cover the coalition politics in the seven States of the region ever since India's independence.

2

DURING THE BRITISH PERIOD

In this Second Lecture an attempt is made to discuss about coalition politics in North-East India during the British period. The term North-East India during this period covered all the territories within the Province of Assam, the Native States of Khasi Hills, Manipur and Tripura. However, for the purpose of this Lecture, the areas will be limited to the existing States of the region barring the areas under the erstwhile Native States as the modern parliamentary system was not introduced by the British in those Native States.

The first territory of North-East India to be annexed by the British East India Company was Assam in 1826 under the Treaty of Yandabo. From 1826 till 1873 Assam was under the Bengal Presidency and without any representative in any legislative or policy making bodies. On February 6, 1874 Assam was constituted into a Chief Commissioner's Province. But there was no legislature and there was no representation of the people of Assam in the running of the government and Administration.[1] For the period from 1874 to 1906 legislative functions for the region were carried on in three ways: Either directly by the Imperial Legislative Council; or by Regulations under 33 Victoria by the Governor General on a proposal from the Chief Commissioner; or by the Chief

Commissioner with the prior sanction of the Governor-General under the Scheduled Districts Act, 1874.[2]

On October 16, 1905 Bengal was partitioned and a new Province of Eastern Bengal and Assam was created. But it was only in 1906 that Assam was allotted two out of 14 seats in the Legislative Council of Eastern Bengal and Assam under the Indian Councils Act, 1892. But even then the local people were not represented. Only two were quasi-elective seats and the rest, mostly Europeans, were nominated by the Lieutenant Governor with the approval of the Governor-General.[3]

It was only under the Indian Councils Act of May 25, 1909 which came into force on November 15, 1909 that Assam got five out of 40 seats. Again, out of five only three were elective seats and the other two went to Industry and one Muslim from the Surma Valley. Hence, the Legislative Council of Eastern Bengal and Assam, though under a non-official majority, did not fully represent the local people.[4] Amalendu Guha has rightly pointed out that: "As a result the local representatives had to look forward to the administration, forging a coalition with the official members, rather than depending on the non-official Indian members".[5] Thus, the seed of coalition politics in North-East India may be said to have started with the Legislative Council of Eastern Bengal and Assam ever since November 15, 1909. One of the reasons for the emergence of such a coalition politics appears to be the "lack of rapport between Eastern Bengal and Assam".[6]

Because of strong opposition to the partition of Bengal, on April 1, 1912 Assam was again reconstituted into its former status of a Chief Commissioner's Province. While the political status of Assam was downgraded, its parliamentary status had been upgraded in the sense that the seats in the Assam Legislative Council which was created in November 1912 under the Indian Councils Act, 1909 had been increased to 25.[7] The non-official members were also in a majority in view of the fact that 15 seats were allotted to them. However, it was a non-Indian Non-Official majority. Indian Members were only 12 in number—six Bengalis, five Assamese and one Parsi. This political situation had resulted in another exercise of coalition politics in the province. The coalition that ensued was generally between the "European Members" and one or two "Indian Official Members". This coalition, according to Guha, "had always an assured majority in the House".[8] The non-official members while standing united could not really form "a stable opposition block".[9]

The process of coalition politics in Assam continued under the Montford Reforms also. On December 23, 1919 the new Government of India Act was passed with the political system known as dyarchy. The Reformed Council, under the new Act, for Assam was constituted in November 1920. The strength of the Council was raised from 25 to 53.[10] Because of the strong opposition to dyarchy, the general elections to the First Reformed Council (1921–23) was boycotted by the nationalists. Inspite of the boycott, out of 53 seats, 33 were elected and the other 20 were nominated officials and non-officials.[11] Here again, there was no majority party; and "a coalition of the European and nominated Indian members formed the government party".[12]

But coalition politics in Assam, in the technical sense, prevailed only during the Second Reformed Council (1924-26). It was during that Council that the Swarajist party with its slogan of wrecking the constitution from within had to seek the support of others as it could secure only eight seats. The natural choice of coalition partners for the Swarajists was for a coalition with other Nationalists and Independents. Thus, the Swarajist-Nationalist-Independent Coalition Party was formed with Faiznur Ali from the Brahmaputra Valley as its leader, and Brajen Narayan Choudhury from the Surma Valley as Deputy Leader.[13]

The Swarajist-Nationalist-Independent opposition coalition was quite successful in its parliamentary performance. It could have its candidate Gopendra Lal Choudhury elected as Deputy President of the Council of March 25 1924. A year later, they had Abdul Hamid elected as President of the Council on March 2, 1925. The coalition was also quite successful in the field of legislative enactments and other legislative business. Guha had, therefore, commented that: "the Second Reformed Council's performance was more impressive than that of the first".[14]

Later on, coalition politics in Assam had undergone some changes in the Third Reformed Council (1927–29). During this council, the Congress Party secured more seats than the Swarajists. But both the groups refused to join the government. In fact, both the parties opposed the formation of any ministry by any other parties, in accordance with the political situation prevailing at that time. The government found it even difficult to get any representation from the two valleys of Assam. It was a very delicate situation when Saadula, a Muslim from the Brahmaputra valley was inducted into the ministry and no Hindu member from the Surma Valley would be willing to accept ministership. This situation paved the way for the induction of Rev. J.J.M. Nichols-Roy, from Shillong General (Urban) Constituency of the Hill Areas into the ministry. The Swarajist-Nationalist coalition continued to operate from the opposition. Even the Independents who had left the Swarajist-Nationalist coalition joined hands with the opposition in defeating the ministry. However, the ministry survived mainly due to the support of the ruling coalition of the solid bloc of the Europeans, both officials and non-officials.[15]

The Fourth Reformed Council (1929–36) had indicated as if the era of coalition politics in Assam was over. But the fact was that it was a period of great political discontent in the country where the functioning of parliamentary democracy was also in a great turmoil. The Swarajists were out and there was no opposition coalition in its absence.[16] It was also a period where the gathering storm of the Second World War and the further development of constitutional reforms took place.

But before we come to the constitutional reforms of 1935, we may have a summary of what was taking place in Assam when parliamentary democracy was introduced in the Province. Before 1921, despite the semblance of popular participation, in fact, the local people were not directly brought into the operational aspect of the parliamentary system. The Head of the Province was not assisted by the Executive Council nor by a Council of Ministers.[17] It was only when the system of dyarchy was introduced in 1921 that the government of Assam consisted of two Executive Councillors for the Reserved subjects and two Ministers for the transferred subjects.[18]

In the First Reformed Council (1921–23) there was no problem in the functioning of the ministry as the Nationalists had boycotted the elections. This had made it much easier for the formation of a coalition between the European members and the Indian nominated members. This coalition formed the government party accordingly.[19] It may be said that it was a coalition government without an opposition. But this does not mean that it could be equated with the concept of a national government.

It was in the Second Reformed Council (1924–26) that the first ever coalition among the opposition parties and groups like the Swarajists, Nationalists, and Independents had been formed. The opposition coalition was so effective that the government was defeated from time to time.[20] It is interesting to note that very much unlike in the present practice of the system of parliamentary government, the defeated government did not resign.[21] The reason was quite simple because the defeat of the government was not through a no-confidence motion.[22] In fact, there was no provision for a no-confidence motion in the Rules framed for the conduct of the Business of the House.[23]

The provision for a no-confidence motion was introduced only in the Third Reformed Council (1926–29) on October 27, 1926. The ministry during the Third Reformed Council was not popular and many no-confidence motions were moved.[24] The first no-confidence motion was moved on February 26, 1927. It was defeated by 27 to 22 votes. The outcome of the no-confidence motion clearly indicated that though the combined elected members or the opposition coalition supported the motion;

the seven officials, six European officials, and some nominated members formed a majority supporting the government. On March 27, 1929, the last day of the Session when the European planters and many Independent members left Shillong, a no-confidence motion was tabled against Rev. J.J.M. Nichols-Roy and the motion was carried by 17 votes in favour to 14 votes against. But Rev. Nichols-Roy did not resign until the Governor-General had to intervene. But Rev. Nichols-Roy resigned as an individual Minister and not the government as a whole.[25]

In the Fourth Reformed Council (1929–36), there was no difficulty in ministry-making as there was no opposition due to the changing political circumstances. As the leader of the national movement were not so much interested in participating in the parliamentary system of government, even the usual tenure of three years for the council continued till the constitutional reforms of 1935.[26]

The new constitutional reforms were introduced under the provisions of the Government of India Act, 1935. Under the 1935 Act, bicameralism was introduced in Assam with the Legislative Council consisting of 22 members as the Upper House, and the Legislative Assembly as the Lower House. The strength of the Legislative Assembly was raised from 53 to 108. This time all the seats in the Legislative Assembly were elective.[27] With the introduction of the Government of India Act, 1935 in Assam in 1937 it may be said that the history of parliamentary system of government in Assam during the last leg of British Rule is the history of coalition ministry-making and coalition ministry-breaking, with all the known patterns of coalition politics having been experimented in the fertile political soil of the Province.

The General Elections to the Assam Legislative Assembly under the new dispensation were held in early 1937. Many political parties took part in the elections. Among others, there were parties like the Congress party, United People's Party, Assam and Surma Valley Muslim Parties (the Muslim League Party, and the United Muslim Party), the Muslim League, Tribal League, European planters and other groups like the Surma Valley Independent Group.[28] Because of the existence of so many political parties, there was a great difficulty in ministry-making as no single political party could command an absolute majority in the House of 108 members. Political instability had become the order of the day as there was no coalition government which would be in a position to command the confidence of the House. No wonder, between 1937 and 1947 there were as many as seven coalition ministries including one Governor's Regime in between. It is to these seven coalitions that we are turning our attention in the following paragraphs.

As we have seen in the 1937 elections, no political party could command a majority. Hence, the first coalition ministry was installed on April 1, 1937 with Saadula as Chief Minister. The coalition partners consisted of the United Muslim Party, Assam Muslim Party, Assam Muslim League, United People's Party, European Group, and Tribal Members.[29] This first coalition ministry, under the Act of 1935, continued until February 4, 1938.[30]

Saadula could become the first Chief Minister as the Congress, the single largest party with 33 members, refused to stake its claim in forming the ministry. It was the European Planters and other allies who acted as the balance of power between the Congress and non-Congress groups. Naturally, due to political compulsion, the balancer leaned heavily towards the non-Congress group and a non-Congress ministry under Saadula was formed with four other ministers—Rohini Kumar Choudhury from the Brahmaputra Valley, Rev. J.J.M. Nichols-Roy from the Hill Areas and two Muslims from the Surma Valley—Abu Nasr Mahmood and Muhammad Ali Hyder Khan. But the coalition was a very weak one as it appeared from its failure to have its candidate elected to the post of Speakership. Instead the Congress candidate B.K. Das from the opposition was elected the Speaker.[31]

With the Speaker, from the opposition, in the Chair, the opposition leader G.N. Bordoloi was in a commanding position. He had, in fact, become quite a formidable force to be reckoned with against the non-Congress coalition ministry. Guha has rightly termed the coalition ministry as "a government without a programme" and "a leaking boat".[32] As a result, Saadula's first coalition ministry had to face a series of defeats in the Assembly which had ultimately paved the way for Saadula's resignation on February 4, 1938.

The problem, however, had arisen after his resignation when the Congress Party refused to form the government. The intra-party and inter-party coalitions in the Legislative Assembly were in such a situation that had enabled Saadula to again form a new coalition ministry the next day on February 5, 1938. His second coalition ministry was further strengthened by increasing the number of his ministers from four to five—R.K. Choudhuri, Rev. Nichols-Roy, two Muslim Leaguers—Abdul Matin Choudhury and Munawwar Ali; and Akshay Kumar Das, a Scheduled Caste member.[33]

The inter-party coalitions both in the ruling and opposition parties were not constant. The fluctuating alignments of inter-party coalitions in the Legislative Assembly had threatened the survival of the second Saadula ministry. While Saadula could win over the Muslim League; G.N. Bardoloi made an attempt to bring about an opposition coalition with the Tribal League particularly of the Plain Areas. His attempt was successful and an agreement with the Tribal League was entered into by the Congress for the formation of an alternative coalition government. This led to the resignation of Saadula's second ministry on September 13, 1938. For about a week Saadula continued with his care-taker coalition government until the Congress and Tribal League coalition was ready to take over power on September 19, 1938.[34]

The Third coalition ministry, which was the first Congress coalition ministry, was formed with G.N. Bordoloi as Chief Minister. There were seven other ministers in the ministry. These were a Tribal League Leader Rupnath Brahma; two Scheduled Caste members Ramnath Das and Akshay Kumar Das; Kamini Kumar Sen; and three Muslims Fakhruddin Ali Ahmed, Ali Hyder Khan, and Mahmud Ali.[35]

But the Congress coalition ministry could not last for long due to the outbreak of the Second World War. Since it was the policy of the Congress Party that all Congress ministries in the country should resign as a protest against the war efforts of the British, the Congress coalition government in Assam was also affected. However, due to non-completion of the immigration policy in the Province, Bordoloi wanted to linger on until his coalition ministry was the last Congress coalition ministry in the country to resign on November 16, 1939.[36]

During the unsettled political situation, for two days, that is between November 15 and 17, 1939 Rev. Nichols-Roy claimed the leadership of the Congress coalition Party. Though he was in the Congress, he was not included in the Bordoloi ministry as the hill people had opposed his inclusion.[37] Though the hill people's opposition was not highlighted but it was quite clear that the anti-British policy of the Congress Party was not yet an accepted principle in the Hill Areas at that point of time. The general attitude of the Hill People during that period was not in favour of the Congress Party to form the ministry. At the same time, from the other political groups, there was a move to prevent Saadula from coming back to power. It was in such a situation that Rev. Nichols-Roy sought the support of the Congress in forming an alternative coalition government with him as the Leader. But the Congress Party did not support him in forming the new Ministry. Instead, Saadula was successful in again forming another coalition ministry under his leadership. The dream of Rev. Nichols-Roy to become the Chief Minister of Assam was thus completely shattered.[38]

Saadula formed his third coalition ministry, which was the fourth in the series of coalition ministries in Assam, on November 17, 1939. This new coalition ministry consisted of nine Ministers. The Ministers were R.K. Choudhuri, Munawwar Ali, Abdul Matin Choudhuri, Rupnath Brahma, Hirendra Chandra Chakravarty, Mudabbi Hussain Choudhuri, Mahendra Saikia, Sayidur Rahman, and Miss. Mavies Dunn. Thus, the strength of the Saadula's third ministry was double of that of his first ministry and bigger than the Bordoloi's ministry, in an attempt to bring about the stability in the coalition government. But inspite of this attempt, Guha remarked that: "The Saadula ministry had an uneasy existence".[39]

There were three main difficulties with the third Saadula coalition ministry. The first was that the Congress Party's anti-war agitation made his coalition government unable to contain the mass movement which was directed mainly against the British Government for its repressive war measures. The second difficulty, ironically, came from the Muslim League. In order to appease the Assamese, the Line System was continued by Saadula but the Muslim League was for its abolition. Saadula was indeed between the devil and the deep sea and his coalition boat was tossing about in the turbulent waters of the war period as well as of the two main communities' attitudes to the Line System in the Province. Saadula had another difficulty, and that is, the survival of his coalition ministry depended mainly upon his continued commitment and support to the British War efforts and the Defence of India Rules to which the Congress Party and the general population of the Province had strongly opposed tooth and nail.[40]

The third Saadula coalition ministry was thus very unpopular. It had to become unpopular since in order to implement the war objectives, repressive measures had to be resorted to. This led to further intensification of anti-war agitations under the leadership of the Congress Party. Saadula had also alienated the Communists and the Leftists when his coalition government had to intern them under the Defence of India Rules. Such kinds of opposition activities and the repressive measures of the coalition government were gradually leading to the building up of a ministerial crisis. The ministerial crisis deepened further when the students of Cotton College were lathi-charged during their anti-war campaign against a week long war-fund raising campaign and scientific exhibition in their college library by the governmental authorities.[41]

Inside the Legislative Assembly too, the third Saadula coalition government had to face a very difficult situation. A number of no-confidence motions were moved. The atmosphere of an aggressive opposition was such that on December 9, 1941 R.K. Choudhuri could no longer remain in the ministry and tendered his resignation accordingly. The ministerial crisis had reached its nadir when on December 12, 1941 Saadula himself tendered his resignation also. He had announced his resignation on the floor of the House the next day on December 13, 1941.

After announcing his resignation, the Treasury Bench staged a walk-out. Normally, the matter should have ended there. But inspite of the walk-out, and that too by the Treasury Bench, the Proceedings of the House continued, and the motion of no-confidence was carried by 56 votes to nil. R.K. Choudhuri along with two Parliamentary Secretaries also voted for the motion. The result had indicated that the opposition was clearly a majority in the House of 108 members.[42] But a more strange political situation was that the Congress Party, after bringing the downfall of Saadula's coalition ministry, was not ready to take over even when it had commanded a coalition majority in the House.[43]

When the Congress Coalition Party refused to form the government, certain attempts were made to find out an alternative government in place of the Saadula's coalition ministry. Like Rev. Nichols-Roy, this time R.K. Choudhuri who had resigned from the Saadula ministry and supported the no-confidence motion against the same ministry sought the support of the Congress Party to form the new ministry. But he could garner the support of only 26 members. True, the Congress Party had assumed of its support from outside excepting its support for war measures. However, the Governor was not satisfied with this kind of support, more particularly on the absence of support for war measures. The British war-efforts being the sine-qua-non for the formation of a new government, and the failure of R.K. Choudhuri to gather sufficient support for an alternative government, the

Governor had no other choice but to exercise his powers under Section 93 of the Government of India Act, 1935. Accordingly, the Governor's Regime was proclaimed on December 25, 1941;[44] and the Saadula care-taker government from November 17, 1941 came to an end the same day. Thus, the dream of R.K. Choudhuri becoming the Chief Minister of Assam, as in the case of Rev. Nichols -Roy, was also shattered.

During the Governor's Rule from December 25, 1941 to August 24, 1942 the government took up certain measures like the scrapping of the Land Development Scheme in order to appease the Hindus and the Assamese of the Brahmaputra Valley. Meanwhile, the Congress party adopted the Quit India Resolution of August 8, 1942. This led, from the beginning of August 10, 1942, to the arrest of prominent Congress leaders and the declaration of the Congress Party and its various organisations as unlawful bodies in the country. The Congress Party being unlawful, a list of eleven prominent Congress functionaries of the Assam Pradesh Congress Committee including the members of the Assam Legislative Assembly was prepared for the purpose of their detention. With their detention, the way was paved for Saadula to come back to power. The British authorities speeded up the process as they sensed that the Governor's rule was unpopular. The "popular resistance" had, therefore, to be met by a "popular ministry". Accordingly, on August 24, 1942 the Governor's Regime came to an end, and the Fourth Saadula Coalition Ministry, which was also called the Muslim League Coalition Ministry, was formed and became the Fifth Coalition Ministry under the Government of India Act, 1935.[45]

The fifth coalition ministry consisted of the same strength as the fourth coalition with 10 ministers including the Chief Minister. The other nine ministers were Munawwar Ali, Abdul Matin Choudhuri, Rupnath Brahma, Hirendera Chandra Chakravarty, Mudabbi Hussain Choudhuri, Mahendranath Saikia, Sayidur Rahman, Mavies Dunn, and Nabakumar Datta. The fourth coalition ministry of Saadula continued the war efforts and pursued the policy of land settlement and immigration. All these measures were against the declared policy of the Congress. Inspite of the strong opposition from the Congress from outside, the Saadula ministry survived till March 23, 1945.[46]

There were many difficulties faced by the fourth Saadula coalition in view of the war conditions and the issues relating to land settlement and immigration. But the prevailing political situation in the Province had enabled him to cling to power till March 23, 1945. It was around that time that the Communist Party of India, taking advantage of the Congress attitude, was extending support to the British war measures and opposing the 1942 August uprisings. Another political development in the Province was that the two-valley district committees of the CPI merged together under one Provincial Committee in May 1943. This merger had to a certain extent helped the CPI to view the political situation in the Province from a more positive angle. After the merger, the CPI appealed to the government to release the national leaders and urged for the Congress-Muslim League Unity to pave the way for the forming of a "national government".[47] The idea of a "national government" was perhaps patterned along the line of the British "national government" during the war years.

The appeal of the CPI did not go in vain. The Congress leaders including Bordoloi and B.K. Das, the Speaker, who hailed from the Surma Valley agreed to the suggestions made by the CPI. The Congress leaders had agreed to such a suggestion because, as Guha has well argued about the fact that the "local considerations in particular weighed heavily in their minds", and that they wanted "to halt the implementation of Saadula's controversial land settlement and immigration policy which had revived since August 1943".[48]

While the Congress Party had its own problems, the Saadula ministry itself was threatened from inside. Saadula himself said to this effect in the Assembly during March, 1945: "The party alignment in the House had been such that the ministry could not carry out its performance and policy for want of a solid majority. As the cabinet was a coalition one, the party majority in the House was very small. The party attachments were mostly fluid. A member was seen sitting on one side of the House at one time and at another place on the same day. This state of affairs was intolerable. Those who had the good of the Province at heart thought that all the parties should join together and draw up an agreed programme and policy and form a cabinet which would command a stable majority".[49] The words used by Saadula in this speech sound similar to the political cliches and jargons used by the political pundits of the present day coalition politics at the national level.

In such a political situation in Assam, both the Congress Party and the Saadula's fourth coalition ministry were approaching towards the goal of mutual understanding. It might be the understanding between two political adversaries but for "the good of the Province". However, before an actual agreement "to join together and draw up an agreed programme and policy", there was an attempt by the Nationalist Coalition Party led by R.K. Choudhuri to wrest power from Saadula. But Choudhuri's second attempt to become the Chief Minister of Assam again failed as he could not command "a stable majority".[50]

It was because of the uneasy war years and the above political developments which had led to an "inevitable existence" of the Saadula's fourth coalition ministry. The pressure on Saadula was gradually but steadily mounting up. The pressure was not only from the Congress Party. But even the Muslim League, for their own reasons, opposed the Government resolution of January 16, 1945 on Wasteland Settlement and the Constitution of Tribal Belts.[51] Naturally, the Saadula's fourth coalition ministry was shaky. After the failure of R.K. Choudhuri to wrest power from Saadula, the Opposition Leader, the leader of the Nationalist Party and the Independent Party met Saadula on March 17, 1945 for the purpose of forming another coalition government.[52] There was even some talk about the possibility of a Saadula-Choudhuri coalition ministry as an alternative to Section 93 of the Government of India Act, 1935. Quite naturally, as an astute politician, Saadula had to seek "fresh allies" for the survival of his ministry.[53]

Saadula had an insight into the working of the mind of the Congress Party and the Choudhuri faction. Hence, in a meeting with the Opposition Leader, the Nationalist and Independent Parties had agreed on March 20, 1945 to step down and form another coalition after his resignation on March 22, 1945.[54] This clearly indicated that Saadula still needed two more days to finally make up his mind. These two days were very crucial indeed as the Congress Party too had to finally make up its mind.

The Congress Party was caught in a situation where it had to look both to the Congress High Command's policy of not taking part in any ministry formation and the local need for "the good of the Province". But the impending collapse of the Saadula's fourth coalition ministry forced the Congress Party to take a final decision. There were three alternative choices for the Congress Party: (a) a Congress coalition ministry; (b) a coalition ministry, without Saadula, but with the support of the Congress from outside; and (c) a coalition ministry headed by Saadula with Congressmen on a minimum programme. These three alternative choices were submitted by Bordoloi to Gandhi on March 14, 1945. The reply came from Gandhi on March 17, 1945 to the effect that Bordoloi could take any of the alternatives which he thought to be the best for the Province.[55] Accordingly, on March 18, 1945, Bordoloi and Choudhuri sent a five-point proposal to Saadula for the reconstitution of the new ministry. On March 19, 1945 Saadula's coalition party agreed to the five-point proposal by a two-thirds majority. The proposal was adopted in order to have a stable ministry. On March 20, 1945 a tripartite agreement was concluded among the three leaders—Bordoloi, Choudhuri, and Saadula to work out the details of the five points which were as follows:

1. the restoration of civil liberties and the gradual release of political prisoners;
2. the suitable policy of procurement and distribution of essential goods, with a view to remove corruption;
3. a revision of the land settlement policy with a view to accommodate claims of the sons of the soil;
4. an agreed distribution of local board seats among the main contending groups; and
5. the reconstitution of the Saadula ministry on an all party basis.[56]

Only after working out the details of the five-point proposal, among the three leaders mentioned above, between March 20–22, 1945 that Saadula agreed to submit his resignation on March 20, 1945. The same day the fifth Saadula coalition ministry, which was the sixth coalition ministry, was formed under the Government of India Act, 1935.[57] The fifth Saadula coalition ministry may be called a grand coalition in view of the fact that it was an all-party coalition acting just as a national government for the people of Assam. But in line with the national political scenario, the Congress Party gave its support from outside and did not join the ministry. To all intents and purposes the Congress Party had adopted the third alternative.

The composition of the new coalition ministry would reflect the policy of the Congress Party at that time. The strength of the new coalition ministry however, remained at 10 as in the two earlier preceding ministries. It included all the five Muslim Ministers, one Tribal Minister from the Tribal groups, and four Hindu Ministers including one member from the Scheduled Caste Community. Apart from Saadula, the other Ministers were Rohini Kumar Choudhuri, Munawwar Ali, Abdul Matin Choudhuri, Akshay Kumar Das, Fakhruddin Ali Ahmed, Mudabbir Hussain Choudhuri, Sayidur Rahman, Baidyanath Mukherjee, and Surendranath Borgohain. It should be noted that since the Congress Party had extended support from outside only, the Congress members did not assume office.

However, all non-Muslim ministers were practically nominees of the Congress Party.[58]

But all was not well with this new arrangement. Tayebullah, the President of the Assam Pradesh Congress Committee, after his release from jail on March 27, 1945 had strongly opposed the Tripartite Agreement. He was not happy that the Congress members should have worked together with Saadula and Choudhuri. According to him these two leaders were war collaborators and the Congress members shouldn't have supported them even from outside. The intra-party conflict continued until the matter reached the Congress High Command in June 1945. However, before the conflict could be resolved, the Second World War came to an end in August, 1945.[59]

In the changed circumstances, therefore, it was pointless for the two factions to pursue the matter further. But Bordoloi, in order to keep the Congress intact, could wriggle out of the bad situation in the party by ending the Tripartite Agreement. The opportunity for ending the Agreement had arisen out of the reason of non-implementation of all the five points by Saadula and that the tenure of the Assembly had also come to an end on October 1, 1945.[60] The Congress-Muslim League coalition or the All-Party Coalition (March 23, 1945 to October 1, 1945) was indeed, as observed by Guha, an "unwise marriage of convenience".[61] With the dissolution of the Legislative Assembly on October 1, 1945 the last Saadula fifth coalition ministry and the last of the six coalition governments under the Government of India Act, 1935 had also come to an end. Saadula's last ministry, however, continued as a care-taker government until February 11, 1946 when the General Elections during the second week of February, 1946 were over.[62]

With the General Elections for the Second Legislative Assembly under the Government of India Act, 1935, the era of coalition politics in Assam during the British period was almost over as the Congress Party had secured an absolute majority. The Congress Party secured 58 seats, Muslim League 31, three Jamiat-ul-Ulema, nine

Europeans, and seven Independent members. But, inspite of a comfortable majority, Bordoloi was cautious in forming the ministry all by the Congress itself. He still preferred to have a coalition ministry. That was why when his ministry took over power on February 11,1946 he included one Muslim Minister from the Jamiat-ul-Ulema and kept two Ministers' seats vacant for the Muslim League though the League did not respond. Later on, Bordoloi included Bhimbar Deuri of the Assam plains Tribal League and Abdur Rashid. Thus, while publicly the Congress Party was committed to the formation of a government on party lines, Bordoloi was still fascinated by the principle of coalition politics. Besides Bordoloi as the Chief Minister, the other Ministers were J.J.M. Nichols-Roy, Ramnath Das, Baidyanath Mukherjee, Basanta Kumar Das, Bishnuram Medhi, Abdul Matlib Majumdar, Bhimbar Deuri, and Abdur Rashid. This position continued till August 14,1947 when the British left India.[63]

Before the British left India, it may be noted that the Bordoloi ministry was a coalition in name only, but a coalition nevertheless. After all, the Jamiat-ul-Ulema as subsequent events would indicate had expressed itself in favour of joining the undivided Assam; and that the Tribal League had joined the Congress Party. The true aspiration of the Assamese leaders was to perpetuate the preponderance of the COngress as well as non- Muslim majority in the Legislative Assembly. That was why the Congress Party had strongly opposed the grouping Scheme of the Cabinet Mission Plan. To further strengthen the opposition to be grouped under Section C with Bengal, there was even "a demand for the self-determination of Assam".[64] In the end, when the partition scheme was announced, Sylhet district, excepting the three thanas of Pathankandi, Ratabari and Badarpur and about one-half of the thana of Karimganj went to join the new State of Pakistan through a referendum and the boundary demarcation under the Redcliff Award.[65]

So far, we have traced how the seed of coalition politics in Assam which was sown on November 15, 1909 in the Legislative Council of Eastern Bengal and Assam had started growing rapidly in the reconstituted Legislative Council of the separate Province of Assam in November 1912. The process of coalition politics had further continued to bloom in the Reformed Councils of the Montford reforms on December 23, 1919 under the new Government of India Act, 1919. The only point to be noted here is that the Legislative Council under the Act of 1919 while consisting of an elected majority, but the official members and the nominated members could manage to have a working majority through the process of a coalition.[66]

But coalition politics in Assam in the technical sense took shape only under the Second Reformed Council (1924–26) when coalition politics came into existence. There were certain changes in the coalition politics during the Third Reformed Council (1927–29) when there were both the ruling and the opposition coalition parties struggling for power. In the Fourth Reformed Council (1929–36) there was an indication of the decline of the process of coalition politics due essentially to the period of great political turmoil and the impending Second World War as well as the absence of opposition parties. But with the formation of the new Legislative Assembly under the government of India Act, 1935 the seed of coalition politics of 1909 which grew up in 1919 and bloomed for over one decade (1924–36) had borne seven coalition fruits. Out of seven coalitions—five were under Saadula and two under Bordoloi between 1937 and 1947. The point to be discussed further is how come that Assam had experienced a series of such coalition politics?

The political configuration in Assam during the British period was essentially a power struggle between the two-valley politics—the Hindus in the Brahmaputra Valley and the Muslims in the Surma Valley. True, there were some Hindu members from the Surma Valley as well as some Muslims from the Brahmaputra Valley. But the Assamese leaders of the Brahmaputra Valley were always cautiously playing their political cards very close to their chest whenever they had to confront any power struggle with the Bengali members of the Surma Valley.

However, it must be said to the credit of the Assamese leaders that if pushed to the wall, they would have preferred a Muslim from the Brahmaputra Valley to become the leader of the House. It was in such a situation that perforce they had to accept the leadership of Saadula, a Muslim from the Brahmaputra Valley to become the Chief Minister of the Province for five times during the decade from 1937 to 1947. It should be noted that Saadula had also been a Minister earlier during the era of the Reformed Council (1927–29).

Another aspect of this power struggle between the two valleys in Assam was the absence of the balancer who would have easily taken over the rein of administration. Rev. J.J.M. Nichols—Roy from the Hill Areas had tried his best but failed to be a balancer as representation from the Hill Areas was smaller in number and could not play an effective role in the game of the balance of power politics, in the Province. Similarly neither the European Planters nor the Tribal League from the Plain Areas would be in a position to play the role of a balancer by themselves separately. True, the European members and the official members bloc tried their best to play the role of a balancer only between the Congress and non-Congress groups and not between the two valleys as such. In the Indian context, even the Indian Statutory Commission had held that: "There was no legislature in which the official bloc was not an actual or potential balancing factor".[67] It was always the official and the nominated non-official members along with either of the two main political groups from the valleys which helped the process of coalition politics in Assam to bear fruit. But this again was possible through the patronage of the British government. This was the political situation at least from 1909 to 1937.

It was only when neither of the two main political groups from the valleys could join hands with the European members as in the Legislative Assembly under the Government of India Act, 1935 that a political vacuum was created into which the Governor of the Province had to step in during the period from December 25, 1941 to

August 24, 1942. Yet, due to heavy political pressures on the Governor during the peak period of the Second World War, attempts were made to bring in a "popular government", be it a coalition government or not. Naturally, only the coalition government could replace the Governor's Rule at that critical juncture. In brief, it had always been the experience of political leaders all over the world that no autocratic regime could be a better substitute for a democratic rule whether in war or peace time conditions.

The various political coalitions in Assam during the British period that had been discussed above had fallen either in one type, pattern, and level of coalition or the other. For example, there was an electoral alliance as in the case of the Assam and Surma Valley Muslim Parties between the Muslim League Party (as differentiated from the Muslim League) and the United Muslim Party during the 1937 elections. Then there were cases of post-election alliances like the Independent Coalition Party (1924–26), the first Saadula coalition ministry (1937–38), the Nationalist Coalition Party of R.K. Choudhuri (1942–45), and the Congress-Tribal League merger (February 1946). The Congress coalition government (1938–39) may be termed as an ideological coalition of like-minded parties like the Tribal League particularly of the Plain Areas. One important feature of coalitions in Assam during the British period was the existence of governmental coalitions in the First (1921–23) and Fourth (1929–36) Reformed Councils where there was no opposition at all.

We may also refer to a Leftist coalition in the sense that the two-valley district committees of the Brahmaputra and Surma valleys had agreed to merge into one Provincial Committee in May 1943. Thus, we have various types of coalitions during the period under study, ranging from legislative, executive, electoral to governmental coalitions. One more type of coalition during the period may also be mentioned and that was the Federal Coalition which may also be called a grand coalition or a responsive coalition, but unlike the governmental coalition, as in the case of the All-Party Coalition or Congress-Muslim

League Coalition under the last Saadula Coalition Ministry (March 1945–October 1945) which continued till the second Congress Coalition which was the seventh and the last coalition ministry under the Government of India Act, 1935 (February 11, 1946–August 14, 1947).

But when all is said and done, coalition politics in Assam did not specifically follow either of the two main theories of coalition. That is, at one time a coalition indicated all the elements of a game theory as in the case of the First two Saadula's coalitions and the first Bordoloi's coalition both depending on the game of numbers. Thereafter, the subsequent coalitions had indicated the elements of a policy-based theory of coalition. The tussle over the immigration policy and the Line System as well as on the Land Development Scheme between the Congress and non-Congress coalitions provided the examples.

A word may also be said about the inter-party and intra-party coalitions in Assam during the British period. It may safely be stated that all the coalition ministries during the period from 1937 to 1947 were all inter-party coalitions. The coalitions before 1937 were different in nature as they were not basically based on party lines; since the parliamentary system of government had not been fully entrenched in the Province. Regarding the intra-party coalitions there was not much literature on such coalitions during the period. But occasional references were made about the existence of intra-party coalitions either among the non-Congress parties or in the Congress Party. The role played by Saadula, R.K. Choudhuri, J.J.M. Nichols-Roy and towards the close of the period by Tayebullah would indicate the existence of such intra-party coalitions in Assam.

Before concluding this second Lecture, it would not be out of place to point out the observations made on the two main political actors who had appeared on the political stage of Assam for over a decade during the crucial period of its history. Lord Wavell, the Vice-Roy, wrote on December 22, 1943 about Saadula in these words: "I saw all the Assam ministers and chief officials, not a very impressive lot, except the Chief Minister, who is a shrewd and competent politician, though how he would do in better company—I am not sure".[68] The stature of Saadula had also been well pinpointed by Guha when he said that because of Saadula's efficiency he could have become a provincial governor and thrive well had he chosen to migrate to Pakistan. But he preferred to stay in Assam and serve his own province after India's Independence.[69]

Not much had been written about Saadula. But we are firmly of the opinion that he knew the politics of the province very well even to the smallest details relating to the self-management system of the Hill People, particularly of the erst-while Khasi Native States. His speeches in the Constituent Assembly of India bear an ample testimony to his quality of head and heart. But that is another story.

On Bordoloi, Sir Robert Reid, the Governor, had observed that he was "a devout Gandhian, honest, obstinate, not very intelligent and with small gift of leadership".[70] But Lord Wavell had a different opinion. He said regarding Bordoloi that he was "a more forcible and quicker intelligent than the Khan Sahib but not a very pleasant personality".[71] It seems that even his own colleagues had misunderstood him. About Bordoloi, Saadula had observed that: "I know Mr. Bordoloi personally. He was my student for a year . . . and then a colleague in the Gauhati Bar. He has been pitchforked into his position by adventitious circumstances. He was not a keen Congressman even and did not go to jail in 1921 or 1931 movements".[72] The fact was that Bordoloi was indeed in jail in 1921.

Not only Saadula from the opposite camp who had made an uncharitable remark against Bordoloi. Tayebullah from the same Congress fold as Bordoloi had also a critical opinion on how much Bordoloi was a Gandhian. Whatever might be the opinions of his colleagues who were from a different cultural background a balanced view has been stressed by Guha that Bordoloi "had enough gift of leadership to have his way at every critical stage, and with popular support. This was so because he could always strike a balance between national and narrowly Assamese interests, as the subsequent events indicated".[73] When one goes through the Proceedings of the Bordoloi Committee for the Assam Tribal and Excluded Areas one is fully convinced that Bordoloi had indeed made an attempt to strike a balance between national and tribal interests as well. But this again is another story.

There were many other political leaders of Assam besides these two prominent leaders who in their own ways had contributed to the richness of the political experience of the province of Assam in coalition politics. The leaders who were on the threshold of freedom could very well see the pros and cons of coalition politics and with their rich experience tried their best to avoid the pitfalls of coalition politics. This was precisely the part played by them in Assam politics during the early days of post-independence India. We shall discuss on how far the political leaders of Assam could achieve their objective in this regard in a much more detailed analysis of the post-independence coalition politics in North-East India in our third and last Lecture in the present series.

3

COALITION POLITICS IN NORTH-EAST INDIA SINCE INDEPENDENCE

In this third Lecture an attempt will be made to trace out the coalition politics prevailing in North-East India ever since India's independence. First of all, a descriptive account of coalition politics in all the seven States of the region will be made. Then, the next step will be to make certain observations on the type of coalitions experimented by these seven political units. Wherever possible an analysis of the process of such coalition politics will also be made. The description of these coalitions will be made in an alphabetical order of the States for the sake of convenience of the members of the audience and not because of any special importance attached to any of the political units.

ARUNACHAL PRADESH

The Scheduled Districts Act of 1874 for Assam was followed by the Assam Frontier Tracts Regulation (Regulation 2) of 1880 which had provided for the exclusion of the Frontier Tracts of Assam from the operation of any governmental enactments in force. The frontier tracts were placed under the Deputy Commissioner of Lakhimpur District as the Political Officer on behalf of the Governor of Assam who looked after their administration as an Agent to the Governor-General of India. The Deputy Commissioner was assisted by the Assistant Political Officer. Between 1882 and 1943 there were four frontier tracts. The first frontier tract to be established was the Dibrugarh frontier tract in November 1882 which was later on known as the Lakhimpur Frontier Tract in the Central Zone. The other three were the Balipara Frontier Tract (Western), Sadiya Frontier Tract (Eastern), and Tirap Frontier Tract (Further East).[1]

After India's Independence, the discretionary powers of the Governor as an Agent to the Governor-General came to an end. He had then to carry on the administration of the frontier tracts and act on the advice of the Chief Minister of Assam.[2] This interim arrangement was again reverted on January 26, 1950 when the discretionary powers of the Governor of Assam were retained and he carried on the administration of the frontier tracts, under the provisions of the Sixth Schedule to the Constitution of India, as an Agent of the President of India.[3] This new constitutional arrangement for the frontier tracts of Assam was just like the system of dyarchy in that the President of India was acting through the External Affairs Ministry while there was no separation from the Tribal Areas Department of Assam until June, 1950.[4]

Thus, there was an anomalous position for about six months so far as the exact nature of the constitutional position of the Assam Frontier Tracts. It took another four years to complete the process of separation of the frontier tracts from Assam under the North-East Frontier (Administration) Regulation, 1954 which had brought about an integrated administration for all the frontier tracts. With the 1954 Regulation all the frontier tracts were brought under the new nomenclature of North-East Frontier Agency (NEFA).[5]

It was on August 1, 1965 that NEFA was transferred from the External Affairs Ministry to the Home Ministry; and in 1967 the NEFA Panchayati Raj Regulation (Regulation 3) was passed. Under this Regulation, a provision was made for an Agency Council at the top of a four-tier system of administration. There was a limited principle of elective elements in the Agency Council which consisted of members like the Member of Parliament from NEFA and the Vice-Presidents of the Zilla Parishads. Gradually, NEFA was renamed Arunachal Pradesh in early 1971 when the Agency Council made a recommendation to that effect.

In the same year, Arunachal Pradesh was constituted into a Union Territory under the North-Eastern Areas (Reorganisation) Act, 1971. The Agency Council was then headed by a Chief Commissioner. The Agency Council used to select a candidate for the Member of Rajya Sabha who was formally nominated by the President of India. For the Member of the Lok Sabha, there was an electoral college of 118 members, who after being elected by these members was formally nominated by the President of India.[6]

Under the new dispensation, the Chief Commissioner appointed five Councillors (Ministers). The indirect system of election was replaced by the system of adult franchise when all the panchayats were all elected bodies. The Agency Council was renamed the Pradesh Council in 1972; and the number of representation to the Lok Sabha was raised to two. The Pradesh Council was converted into a Provincial Legislative Assembly in 1975 with 30 members, and the then existing five Councillors became a Provisional Council of Ministers headed by Prem Khandu Thungon as the first Chief Minister of Arunachal Pradesh. The other four Ministers were Tomo Riba, Sobeng Tayeng, Tadar Tang, and Wangpha Lawang.[7]

The First General Elections in Arunachal Pradesh was held in 1978. There were two main political parties, the Janata Party and the People's Party of Arunachal (PPA). The Janata Party came into existence in Arunachal Pradesh due to the trend of: "Joining and rejoining the ruling or prospective ruling party at the Centre by State units of national parties and the regional parties".[8] In the 1978 Elections, the Janata Party secured an absolute majority of 17 members in the House of 30 members followed by PPA with eight members and five Independents.[9] The Congress party drew a blank. Later on, three more members were nominated to the Assembly and further strengthened the Janata Party which came to power with P.K. Thungon as Chief Minister on March 14, 1978. But because of defection Thungon had to resign and Tomo Riba of the PPA along with some defectors and Independents formed a short-lived ministry of only about two months from September 18, 1979. Before Tomo Riba's fell from power, Gegong Apang, who by then had aligned himself with the Congress (I) made an attempt to form an alternative government but failed to achieve his objective. This was followed by the imposition of President's Rule in Arunachal in November, 1979.[10]

It is not very clear whether Tomo Riba had formed a coalition ministry or not. But considering the fact that his PPA had only eight members with the support of those who had joined with his party either as defectors or independently, then it would be appropriate to call it a coalition ministry. Similarly, after Riba's government fell from power due to redefection, Gegong Apang also tried to unsuccessfully form another coalition ministry. In which case, it may be said that Tomo Riba's ministry was the first coalition ministry in Arunachal Pradesh after the system of direct election was introduced in the Union Territory, even if it was run under the umbrella of a regional party. At most, it was an intra-party coalition because of defection from other parties and groups to and aligning with the PPA.

The next General Elections in 1980 after a short spell of President's Rule in November 1979 brought the two main political parties, the PPA and the Congress Party as serious contenders for power in the Union Territory. Both parties secured 13 seats each with four Independents.[11] Though the PPA secured 41.52 per cent of votes against 37.74 per cent polled by the Congress Party, yet the latter could form the government, again because of defection of some members including the Independents. The ministry led by Gegong Apang in 1980 also fell under the same category as the previous one led by Tomo Riba. Hence, it could also be categorised as a coalition government though under the umbrella of the Congress Party.

Ever since the 1980 elections, the Congress Party had been able to retain its dominance in the 1984 elections with 21 seats; and in the 1990 elections as well when Arunachal Pradesh was raised to the status of a State (1987) with 60 members in the Legislative Assembly winning 37 seats. The PPA which had joined the Janata Dal during the National Front Government at the Centre could bag only 11 seats. The dominance of the Congress Party was further strengthened with another trend in the State politics: "A strong tendency on the part of the opposition MLAs to join the ruling party in the State as soon as the election is over, irrespective of their previous party affiliations".[12]

The last General Elections to the State Assembly were held on March 11, 1995. There was no opposition party in the State since the PPA turned Janata Dal during 1990 and the other opposition members joined the Congress Party either as full or, associate members. But then, it was the rebel Congressmen who had posed a challenge to the Congress Party. These rebel Congressmen hurriedly organised the Janata Dal and the Janata Party. To these two parties from among the rebel Congressmen, the Bharatiya Janata Party (BJP) also made a second attempt (the first was in 1984 and skipping over the 1990 elections), and a large number of 102 Independents took part in the elections. Inspite of the intra-party differences, the Congress came out successfully with 43 seats followed by 12 Independents.[13] But after the parliamentary elections (both for the Lok Sabha and the Rajya Sabha) in 1996, due partly to intra-party differences and mainly because of the foreigners' issue, Gegong Apang, the Chief Minister resigned from the Congress Party and formed a new party, the Arunachal Congress on September 20, 1996.[14] The Congress (I) ministry in the State had, thus, become over-night the Arunachal Congress ministry.

In such a situation, it is very difficult indeed whether to call the Arunachal Congress ministry a grand coalition ministry in as much as all the Assembly members of the Congress (I) had also become the Assembly members of the Arunachal Congress. Technically, it may be called a coalition in view of the fact that the Arunachal Congress members were earlier elected as the Congress(I) candidates and not as the Arunachal Congress candidates. It is a clear case of merger, if not defection, from one party to another to form a new government. The fact, however, remains that unlike other States of North-East India "party politics in the State moves round the ruling party at the Centre and the State".[15] That is the reason why the Arunachal Congress supported the BJP led coalition government at the Centre after the 1998 parliamentary elections.

ASSAM

Assam had been under the Congress ministries since India's independence till 1978. But, as has already been pointed out in Part-II of the Lecture, immediately after independence there was a sort of a coalition government under the Congress which was continued from the Bordoloi's ministry of February 1946. Gradually, the Congress Party took over the government by itself and continued to rule the State for three decades, excepting for the period during 1958–60 when the East India Tribal Union (EITU) joined the Congress ministry as a matter of political expediency. However, when we discuss about coalition politics we do not really confine ourselves only to the ruling party side. We have also to look into the process of coalition politics in the opposition camp. We propose to do so in the following five paragraphs for the period from 1952 to 1978 when the Congress Party was the single dominant party in the State.

During the period from 1952 to 1956 there were attempts for pre-poll alliances among various non-Congress parties. The Forward Bloc, Bloshevik Party, Revolutionist Socialist Party and the Communist Party of India (CPI) tried to form the United Progressive Front but could not materialise.[16] The Socialist Party, the Forward

Bloc (Ruiker Group), and the Kisan Mazdoor Praja Party (KMPP) also tried to forge an alliance but failed.[17] The attempt for a pre-poll alliance was successful only between the Socialist Party and the Tribal Sangha.[18] There were also local electoral alliances as among the Cachar Communist Party and the KMPP where the Communists supported the KMPP candidates in the Hailakandi and Karimganj constituencies.[19] Similarly, in Dibrugarh, the KMPP supported the Communist candidate in Dibrugarh East constituency and the Communists supported the KMPP in other constituencies.[20] But after the General Elections of 1952 and during the period of the First Assembly under the new Constitution of India there was the United Opposition Bloc. This coalition of opposition parties in the State Assembly consisted of the CPI, the Socialist Party, the KMPP and some Independents.

Before the 1957 General Elections there was an electoral alliance among the Praja Socialist Party (PSP), the Socialist Party and the CPI.[21] There were also local pre-poll alliances as in Gauhati constituency when the PSP and the Revolutionary Communist Party of India (RCPI) did not set up candidates against the Communist Party candidate, Gauri Shankar Bhattacharya. Another local pre-poll alliance was in Rampur constituency where the Communists did not set up their candidate against Hareswar Goswami. Similarly, in Amguri constituency, the Communist Party and the PSP did not set up candidates against the RCPI candidate, Khagendra Nath Barbarua.[22]

The purpose of the pre-poll alliance among these different parties was naturally to defeat the Congress Party. When their purpose was not achieved they did not even form a united opposition in the House.[23] After the 1962 General Elections, however, the opposition parties being very weak with 26 members only, even without a pre-poll alliance had to resort to a post-poll alliance by forming an opposition coalition. The opposition coalition was named the United Opposition Front, at different times, consisting of the PSP, RCPI, the All Party Hill Leaders' Conference (APHLC), and the Independents.[24]

In the 1967 General Elections, the opposition parties had improved their position by doubling their membership over their 1962 performance. Yet, instead of having one united opposition coalition there were two instead. The one called the United Legislature Party under the leadership of G.S. Bhattacharya consisted of 22 members including the Independents; and the other was the United Democratic Front with 20 members under the leadership of the CPI veteran, Phani Bora. The APHLC with nine members constituted an opposition group only having failed to get the required number of 18 for being recognised as an opposition Party.[25]

In 1972, after the opposition's debacle with 19 opposition members only had to form one opposition coalition after the General Elections. The opposition coalition was called the Opposition Front consisting of the CPI, the Socialist Party, and the United Legislature Party of the People's Democratic Party and the Independents. The Swatantra Party, however, had stayed away from the ULP.[26] Thus, from 1952 to the next General Elections in 1978, the opposition parties, inspite of their various attempts for a strong and effective coalition, had miserably failed to dislodge the Congress Party from power in Assam. The opposition parties could have easily exploited the weakness of the State Congress Party had it not been for the strength of the Congress Party at the Centre. In the next three paragraphs an attempt will be made to find out the intra-party coalitions within the Congress Party.

Within the Assam Pradesh Congress Committee (APCC) there were intra-party coalitions from time to time. While the opposition parties had some understanding among themselves to fight against the Congress Party, the latter "had to fight a sort of warfare within its ranks".[27] This was not the case with the 1952 elections only. In fact, there were four intra-party coalitions in the APCC ever since Bordoloi's time. Debeswar Sarma was personally anti-Bordoloi, vying for Chief Ministership; Bishnuram Medhi with his provincial outlook opposed Bordoloi's accommodation of the minorities and tribal people;

Motiram Bora nursed his personal ambition for not being included in the Bordoloi's ministry in the early part of ministry-making; and the group of members, who were influenced by the Assam Mahasabha, putting communal pressure on Bordoloi.[28]

But Bordoloi could still keep the Congress Party intact till he passed away from the scene. Then "in the elections of 1957 some elements were indirectly working against Bishnuram Medhi".[29] In the contest for leadership, Medhi won by only a small margin of six or seven votes.[30] But the anti-Medhi intra-party coalition was so strong enough in influencing the Congress High Command for bringing in a new leader. It was in such a situation that an outsider to the House, Bimala Prasad Chaliha, was brought in as the new Chief Minister of Assam.

Chaliha was re-elected in 1962, but another intra-party coalition led by Dev Kanta Baruah made an attempt in 1965 to outset Chaliha "for their personal and political differences".[31] After this intra-party difference, not much intra-party coalition in the Congress Camp could be noticed from 1966, and the Congress Party managed to run the government of the State till 1978. But by that time (1969–71) and onwards there was a split in the Congress Party at the Centre which had produced a similar split in the APCC. Besides, the Congress Party at the Centre had been defeated in the 1977 Lok Sabha polls and the Janata Party had come to power. It is to be seen whether the non-Congress parties in Assam could make the best out of the changing political situation.

The result of the 1978 General Elections to the Assam Assembly which were held on February 25, 1978 produced a result where no political party could command a majority. The Congress which had ruled the State for three decades suddenly found itself in a minority and resigned on March 3, 1978. The following were the results:

Janata Party =	53	PTCA	=	4
Congress (R) =	26	RCPI	=	4

CPI (M)	= 11	Independents =	15	(including Socialist Unity Council of India
Congress (I) =	8			(SUCI) = 2; and
CPI = 5				CPI – ML = 1)
		Total	=126	

The Janata Party, as the single largest party, would have to find out coalition partners in order to enable it to form a coalition ministry.[32] The Janata Party could form the second coalition ministry after India's independence with the help and support of four PTCA members and five Independents (styled Popular Democratic Front) excluding the SUCI and CPI (ML). The CPI (M) with 11 members supported the coalition ministry from outside making a total of 73 members in the House of 126.[33] Rao and Hazarika gave the figure of two additional members who had defeated from the Congress (R).[34] The Janata coalition ministry was led by Golap Barbora of the Janata Party. Barbora's ministry was called the second coalition because the first coalition government in Assam, after independence, in fact took place during the Chaliha's Congress ministry when the EITU, the forerunner of the APHLC, joined the Congress ministry (1958–60) as a partner.[35]

Golap Barbora had very difficult times in keeping his ministry intact. One reason was internal, because of political unrest in the State and the foreigners' problem arising out of the Lok Sabha bye-election to the Mangaldai parliamentary constituency due to the passing away, on March 20, 1979, of Hiralal Patwari of the Janata Party. Another reason was the break up of the Janata coalition government at the Centre on July 15, 1979 due to the split in the Janata Party on July 10, 1979 into Janata Party and Janata Secular Party (Janata–S), a combination of a majority of the Bharatiya Lok Dal (BLD) and two other groups under the leadership of Raj Narain.[36]

After the resignation of Morarji Desai on July 15, 1979, Charan Singh formed another coalition ministry on July 28, 1979 with the help of the Congress (U). In passing, it may be noted that in 1978, the Congress (I) again had another split with the Congress (B) of Brahmana Reddy which became the Congress (S) of Swaran Singh in 1979, and the Congress (U) of Devraj Urs. Of course, by 1981, the Election Commission declared the Congress(I) as the real Congress.[37] Meanwhile, the Charan Singh coalition ministry failed to face the no-confidence motion and resigned on August 20, 1979 and the Lok Sabha was dissolved two days later on August 22, 1979.[38]

It was under such circumstances that the Janata Party in Assam found itself in a very difficult situation. Like the Congress split of 1969–71 which had its effects in Assam, the Janata split (1979) at the Centre had similar effects in the State too. Barbora had aligned himself with Morarji Desai who was supported by the Jan Sangh which later on turned into the Bharatiya Janata Party (BJP) on April 6, 1980. On June 22, 1979 Barbora tried to reconstitute his ministry; but on June 30, 1979 the Janata-S group was formed in the Assam Assembly by A.F.G. Osmani, Zahir-ul-Islam, Mohammad Ali Choudhury, and Abdus Subham. This new political development precipitated the reconstitution of the new ministry by dropping three Cabinet Ministers and one Minister of State on July 13, 1979.[39]

The second coalition ministry of Golap Barbora was sworn in on July 14, 1979 but four Ministers-designate did not attend; and on July 18, 1979 two Cabinet Ministers Jagannadh Sinha and Keshab Chandra Gogoi resigned from the Ministry while still remaining in the party. These two Ministers had levelled charges against Barbora "for misusing administrative machinery and stalling developmental activities".[40] But inspite of dismissal of Ministers, absence of Ministers-designate in the swearing-in ceremony, and the subsequent resignation of his Ministers, Barbora could still retain 68 members including seven Associate Members. The party position at this critical juncture was:[41]

Janata Party	= 57	PTCA	=	4
Congress (U)	= 23	RCPI	=	4
CPI (M)	= 11	SUCI	=	2

Congress (I) =	8	CPI (ML) =	1
CPI =	6	Independents =	6
Janata (S) =	4		
		Total =	126

The following day, on August 19, 1979 Dr. Tarani Mohan Barua announced that a group of 17 Janata members had withdrawn their support to Barbora; and also claimed to have the support of 23 Congress (U) members led by Sarat Chandra Sinha. Dr. Barua went ahead and formed the Assam Janata Dal (Tarani's group) with 21 MLAs. He further claimed that five more Janata MLAs had also left the Janata Party, thus reducing its membership to 42 only. Further, six Independents formed the Progressive Democratic Front (PDF) and withdrew their support from Barbora. The Speaker, Jojendra Hazarika, then informed the Governor that 18 Janata MLAs had resigned from the Janata Party. Thus, in one day only, many political changes had taken place in the State politics of Assam which had shaken the Janata coalition ministry of Barbora.[42]

The next day, that is, on August 20, 1979 Dr. Barua informed the Governor that he had the support of 70 MLAs and requested him to summon the Emergency Session of the Assembly for a trial of strength. The AJD of Dr. Barua with Jogendra Hazarika as the leader of the Dal had received the support, from outside, of the Congress(U) and the Congress (I) thus reaching a majority of 64 members. In addition, there was also the unconditional support of the CPI (M). Accordingly, on September 3, 1979 a no-confidence motion against the Janata coalition ministry of Barbora was moved by Giasuddin Ahmed of the CPI and eight other opposition parties. The no-confidence motion was admitted and scheduled for a discussion on September 4, 1979. But before the no-confidence motion could be taken up Barbora tendered his resignation.[43] The *Statesman* had very neatly summed up the fall of Barbora's ministry in the following words:

"What sounded its (i.e. Barbora's ministry's) death-knell, however, was local communalism, which was exacerbated by tension in New Delhi between Janata and Janata–S factions. Mr. Barbora was imprudent enough to yield to pressure and dropped two Muslim Ministers, Mr. Goolam Osmani and Mr. Zahir-ul-Islam. This played right into the hands of the dissidents. Who, with an astute eye on the ostensible rationale of the split in New Delhi, at once ran up the standard of secularism, opted for Mr. Charan Singh and accused the Chief Minister of pandering to religious bigotry. Their cause was further strengthened when Mr. Barbora tried (unwisely in political terms) . . . to take a firm line on illegal immigration from East Bengal, which has always been something of a way of life for Assam. . . ."[44]

The result was that another coalition ministry in Assam was formed on September 9, 1979 under the Chief Ministership of Jogendra Hazarika. The ruling coalition party position at that time was:[45]

AJD	=	17	(also called Assam Janta Vidayini Dal).
CPI	=	6	
Associate Members (AJD)	=	9	(later on Hazarika claimed on December 12, 1979 that three members of Janata–S or Lok Dal as Associate Members of AJD).
Congress (I)	=	8	
Independent	=	1	
Total	=	63	(later on raised to 68 members).[46]

The position of the CPI (M) and Janata (S) was not clear at that time. But CPI (M) did criticise the CPI and Congress (I) for having supported Hazarika's coalition ministry. But T.S. Murty has rightly pointed out that the criticism of the CPI (M) for CPI's role in Assam coalition politics where the Congress (I) was involved was not different from the role played by the CPI (M) in supporting the Charan Singh's coalition ministry at the Centre which was also supported by the Congress (I).[47] And regarding the Janata (S) as has already been indicated above, Hazarika later on claimed that three Janata (S) members had become Associate Members of the AJD.[48]

In passing, it may be noted that between September 4, 1979 when Barbora resigned and September 9, 1979 when Hazarika took over there was an alternate attempt for a New Janata coalition ministry on September 6, 1979 consisting of the Janata Party, RCPI, PTCA, and CPI (ML). This proposed alternate coalition was very hopeful of the support of the CPI (M), SUCI, and some Independents. In fact, the CPI (M) had even informed the Governor that they might agree to the formation of such a coalition government. But the proposed coalition later on proved to be a failure,[49] and Hazarika was successful in forming the third coalition ministry in the Sixth Assam Assembly.[50]

However, the third coalition ministry under the leadership of Hazarika had to face a very rough political weather due to agitational politics organised by the All Assam Gana Sangram Parishad (AAGSP or alternately AGSP). The AGSP was formed on August 27, 1979, that is, two weeks before the assumption of office by Hazarika. In fact, the agitations were directed against the Hazarika coalition ministry. Inside the House also, Hazarika had to face a no-confidence motion on November 11, 1979 but fortunately for him the motion was defeated. The party position at that time was:[51]

Janata Party	=	32	PTCA	=	4
Congress (U)	=	22	RCPI	=	4
AJD	=	19	SUCI	=	2
CPI (M)	=	11	Independents	=	2
Congress (I)	=	9	CPI (ML)	=	1
Janata (S)	=	7	Vacancies	=	2
CPI	=	6			
PDF	=	5	Total	=	126

One week later, the agitational programmes were intensified from November 19, 1979. The preparation for the Lok Sabha General Elections was disturbed due to the boycott on the part of the All Assam Students Union (AASU) and the AGSP. Meanwhile, the CPI was unhappy with Hazarika; and on December 11, 1979 the Congress (U) withdrew its support followed by the resignation of 11 Ministers and two Parliamentary Secretaries under the leadership of K.C. Gogoi. As a result, the political situation became so confused that it was not possible to ascertain about the fate of the Hazarika coalition ministry nor the formation of any winning majority-coalition or otherwise.[52] In fact, there were three alternative choices:[53]

1. Hazarika still claimed a majority-coalition which he could not prove;
2. K.C. Gogoi wanted to form a coalition ministry with the Janata and the Communists which could not be confirmed; and
3. Some members claimed that they could form a New Assam Janata Dal coalition government backed by the Janata Party and the Congress which could not be ascertained.

In such a confused political situation, on December 12, 1979 the Governor of Assam sent a report to the Centre that the constitutional machinery in the State had broken down; and on the same day the President's Rule was proclaimed in the State under Article 356 of the Constitution.[54] Thus, the third Assam coalition ministry during the Sixth Assembly came to an end.

There were three other attempts at coalition ministry-making immediately after the President's Rule was clamped on December 12, 1979. The first one was on December 13, 1979 when the Janata Party, Congress (U) and AJD tried to form an alternate coalition ministry. Having failed to form such an alternate coalition ministry, the second attempt for the formation of a coalition government six days later, that is, on December 19, 1979 by the Janata Party, Congress (U), RCPI and the PTCA (on the condition that the new State of Udayachal be created). These four parties would like to work out a common minimum programme.[55]

However, before they could achieve their objective, the difference of opinion on the cut-off year of 1951 on the foreigners' issue brought about a deadlock among the Janata Party, PTCA and RCPI on the one side, and the CPI (M), CPI, and Congress (U) on the other. The latter would prefer to fix March 23, 1979 as the cut-off date. But, the difference, in fact, had arisen because (a) the Congress (U) High Command, on December 27, 1979, had expressed that it was not in favour of a coalition government at that time, and if it were to be done it should be at the APCC (U)'s and S.C. Sinha's own risk; and (b) the PTCA till December 28, 1979 had yet to receive the response from the Janata Party on the question of Udayachal.[56]

The third attempt at coalition-making was made on the same day, that is, on December 28, 1979 by Dr. Barua of AJD who had staked his claim for Chief Ministership of a new coalition government with AJD, CPI, CPI (M), and Lok Dal (former Janata-S). This attempt, again, could not materialise.[57]

Meanwhile, Indira Gandhi came to power at the Centre on January 14, 1980. The new Congress Government at the Centre felt that it was its responsibility to conduct the parliamentary elections in Assam which were boycotted by the people of Assam, excepting in Silchar, Karimganj and Autonomous Districts parliamentary constituencies. But its main responsibility was to contain the agitational programmes that had been continuing in the State. To achieve these twin objectives, Indira Gandhi was in favour of having a Congress (I) ministry in the State before the end of one year of President's Rule as per provision of Article-356(5) of the Constitution. The President's Rule was accordingly revoked on December 6, 1980. On the same evening of December 6, 1980 the Congress (I) government under the Chief Ministership of Mrs. Sayida Anwar Taimur was formed. It was not a majority but simply a single largest group ministry.[58]

Though the Taimur's ministry was the Congress (I) ministry, yet in our view it was a coalition ministry in as much as there was a support from other parties from outside without ever joining it. This had been proved by the fact that though the Congress (I) minority government had only 45 members in the House of 121 (five vacancies), it was supported by 28 more members of the CPI (M), CPI, Lok Dal, Congress (U), SUCI, RSP and RCPI by promising not to topple the Congress (I) ministry. That had brought in the majority number of 73 members.[59] Thus, the Taimur Congress (I) ministry was clearly a minority government, and if not a coalition ministry, at least it fell under the category of legislative coalition because of the legislative support of the other 28 members in the House.

The problem for the Taimur's ministry, however, started to surface out from the dissidents of the Congress (I) party itself. By March, 1981 there were only 44 Congress (I) members. Taking advantage of the rumblings within the Congress (I) fold, the United Opposition of the S.C. Sinha's Congress (U), Golap Barbora's Janata, and Jogendra Hazarika's AJD made an all out attempt to form an alternative coalition government in the event of the fall of the Taimur's ministry. To speed up its downfall, there were six no-confidence motions by the Janata Party, Congress(U), PTCA, Lok Dal, and PDF separately on March 19, 1981 which were taken up for a discussion on March 24, 1981. The motion was, however defeated when 23 Leftist members abstained from voting. Only 44 members voted for the motion. The 44 members included the following:

Janata Party	=	27	Lok Dal	=	1
AJD	=	4	CPI (ML)	=	1
PICA	=	4	Independents	=	3
Congress (U)	=	3			
BJP	=	1	Total	=	44

At this time the Congress (I) had 54 members but six of them remained neutral and the Taimur's ministry was saved by the remaining 48 members as against 44 opposition members who had voted for the motion.[60] The success of the Taimur's ministry was, however, short-lived. It was again because of the infighting or intra-party coalitions within the Congress (I) camp which had brought about the political instability in the ministry and in the State as well. By April 28, 1981 the Congress (I) dissidents under the leadership of Altaf Hussain Majumdar, the Tea-Garden group under Nagbansi and others grew to 22 members. Here again, there was a short-lived reprieve for the Taimur's ministry when Dr. T.M. Barua (then an Independent) and three Janata leaders (Kul Bahadur Chhatri, Razi Kutubbudin Ahmed and Abdul Kayum Choudhury) joined the Congress (I) making its total number between 44 to 46 only.[61] Subsequently, on June 22, 1981 eight Congress (I) under Altaf Husain Majumdar went to Delhi with a demand for a change in the Congress (I) leadership in the State. Simultaneously, 23 members of the Left Front Alliance and four PTCA ceased to lend their support to the Taimur's ministry bringing a total of 35 members opposing the ministry. Taimur had no other alternative but to tender her resignation on June 28, 1981;[62] and the fourth coalition ministry of the Sixth Assembly came to an end. Having no possibility of any other alternative government, the President's Rule was again imposed in the State on June 30, 1981 till January, 1982.[63]

In between the President's Rule, there was tussle between K.C. Gogoi who succeeded Taimur with 44 members of the Congress (I) with a claim of the support of 63 members in the 118-member House (eight vacancies) on the one side, and S.C. Sinha of the Congress (U) who claimed the support of 65 members on the other. While these claims and counter-claims went on, the President's Rule was revoked on January 13, 1982;[64] and on the same day, K.C. Gogoi was sworn in as the Chief Minister of the Congress (I) ministry. The strong reaction of the Left Democratic Alliance was immediate and condemned the Government of India's action as a "dirty act" and demanded the dismissal of the Gogoi's ministry. In fact, the Left Democratic Alliance had 67 members (Janata—27; Leftists—23; Congress(U)—3; Lok Dal —1; AJD—2; CPI(ML)—1, and Independents—10).[65] Yet the stronger reaction was to come from the AASU and AGSP which called the installation of the Gogoi's ministry as an "illegal installation of a government with defectors and legislators elected on foreigners' votes".[66]

But for our purpose, the question is whether the Gogoi's ministry was a coalition or not, our view is that it was a coalition ministry in the sense that though the

Congress (I) had only 46 members, it claimed the support of four PTCA members and 11 Independents bringing a total of 61 members in the 118-member House (eight vacancies).[67] Since its claim was not acceptable to the opposition members, a no-confidence motion was moved on March 17, 1982 by eight members of Sinha's Congress (U), Barbora's Janata, Hemen Das' CPI(M), and Promod Gogoi's PDF. K.C. Gogoi tried to gain support for his ministry but had miserably failed to do so, and had to resign on March 19, 1982.[68] With this the fifth and the last coalition ministry of the Sixth Assembly came to an end. In that context, the Gogoi's ministry may, therefore, be called a non-responsive coalition and did not fall under any pattern, level, kind or type of coalitions as discussed in Part - I of these Lectures. After the resignation of the Gogoi's coalition ministry, the Assembly was dissolved the same day, that is, on March 19, 1982 and the President's Rule was again imposed in the State till the coming to power of the Congress ministry under Hiteswar Saikia (1985); the non-Congress ministry of the AGP under Prafulla Kumar Mahanta (1986); and again the Hiteswar Saikia's Congress ministry (1991).

So, for about ten years there was a period of almost a closed chapter on coalition politics in Assam excepting when the AGP due to internal infighting had to make certain adjustments with some other groups like the Autonomous State Demand Committee (ASDC) similar to the adjustment between the Chaliha's ministry and the EITU in the late fifties. This kind of coalition is called the governmental coalition because the single party can run its government even without the support of any other party. But for political expediency, certain parties are admitted to the privilege of power-sharing in the State apparatus.

The next coalition politics in Assam can be seen again during the 1996 General Elections to the State Assembly. Before the elections in May 1996,[69] the AGP had a pre-poll alliance and the adjustment of seats with four other political parties in the State. The AGP as the major partner had contested only 99 out of 119 seats (other seven seats were out of the initial polling schedule); CPI(M)—2; CPI—3; ASDC—5; and the United People's Party of Assam (UPPA) as an Independent—1. AGP won 59 seats; CPI(M) retained—2; while CPI lost one and ASDC gained one over the 1991 elections respectively. The party position in the Tenth Assembly (1996) was as follows:[70]

AGP	=	59	CPI	=	2	(Barua mentioned 3)
Congress (I)	=	34	CPI(M)	=	2	
ASDC	=	5	Independents	=	11	(including UPPA)
BJP	=	4				
AICC(T)	=	2	Total	=	119	(Mahanta contested Berhampur and Nowgong seats; and vacated his home constituency of Nowgong).

The AGP pre-poll pact with the four other parties had brought about the "unity of the opposition camp" and the "avoidance of any major division of votes".[71] This had enabled the AGP, though with no majority, to form the coalition ministry with other parties. The swearing-in ceremony of the AGP coalition ministry, with P.K. Mahanta as Chief Minister was on May 15, 1996. He included in his 28-member ministry the CPI veteran Promod Gogoi, and Abdul Muhib Majumdar of the UPPA. As a governmental coalition, the Mahanta ministry had commanded a majority. Besides, the ASDC and the CPI(M) had also extended their support from outside.

Thus, Mahanta's coalition ministry (1996) combined the pre-poll coalition, the governmental coalition, and the legislative coalition. But of late, there was an intra-party coalition in the AGP leading to internal dissension. In order "to quell rebellion by a motley group of AGP dissidents in May 1998", Mahanta had to expand his ministry to 32. The dissidents in the AGP camp were quite formidable and they "were led by former PWD

Minister, Atul Bora and Mahanta's confident turned foe Bhrighu Kumar Phukan".[73] It is yet to be seen how the AGP coalition ministry would face the ever changing political situation in the State in the next remaining three years of the Tenth Assembly (1996–2001).

MANIPUR

Towards the close of the eighteenth century during the reign of Raja Jai Singh upto 1789 the Burmese had made further inroad into Manipur. It was then that the British assistance was sought by the Raja but the former could reach only upto Kashipur in Cachar. But in 1823 when the Burmese had a head on clash with the British in Cachar, the British made an alliance with Raja Gambhir Singh. After the Anglo-Burmese War of 1823–26 by the Treaty of Yandabo 1826 Gambhir Singh was declared a semi-independent ruler of Manipur.[74] Till 1850 the British policy towards Manipur was one of indifference. It was only during the region of Raja Chandra Kirti Singh, because of his shaky position, that the British took advantage of the situation and took control over Manipur Semi-independent status while allowing it to maintain its internal autonomy. Anti-British activities then started appearing ever since 1886 when Senapati Tikendrajit Singh was the real ruler of Manipur and Raja Sura Chandra Singh was concerned only with religious observance.[75]

The anti-British activities of Tikendrajit Singh was suppressed by the British during the Anglo-Manipur War of 1890–91. Subsequently, a transitional arrangement was made to exercise the supreme authority of the State by a Political Officer making the Raja totally subservient to the British.[76] When Chura Chand Singh became the Raja of Manipur on May 15, 1907 the British had made it clear in the *sanad* that he must obey any order issued by the Government of Assam. Further, to curb his power a Darbar was constituted consisting of members to be appointed with the approval of the Assam Government where one member of the Assam Service was also included.[77] Besides the Maharaja as the President, the

Darbar consisted of the Vice-President (an ICS Officer from the Government of Assam), and six nominated Manipuris. Since 1916 the Maharaja had preferred to have only a supervisory control over the Darbar and allowed the Vice-President to be the President.[78]

The State Darbar was a very important institution where the seed of a coalition administration was carried on between the British component and the Manipur representation. As a result there was an "anomalous position" when the Maharaja was assisted in the administration of the State and on the other hand the Maharaja could veto any resolution of the Darbar and might pass any order he so wished. But a more serious situation could arise if the Maharaja and the President (a British Officer) of the State Darbar had any difference of opinion. Either the President had to concede to the veto power of the Maharaja or had to refer the same to the Governor of Assam as the Agent to the Crown Representative. Hence, the veto power of the Maharaja over the Darbar was withdrawn excepting for the veto power over the President's action. This was another "anomalous position" in the coalition set up of the Darbar. Of course, because of the Second World War situations the restrictions on the Maharaja were withdrawn in 1943. But by that time the future of the Native States in the new constitutional set up of India was already hanging in the balance.[79]

In November 1946 when the end of British Paramount over Manipur was in sight, the Governor of Assam had completely changed the British attitude towards the State. The rigorous imperialist conditions of the 1891 *sanad* had been moderated for a more conciliatory attitude. The supportive role of the Maharaja to the British during the war time, when the Japanese were knocking at the door of Imphal, could be one of the reasons for such a change in the British would not have liked that Manipur be integrated with India.[80]

When India was on the threshold of freedom, there were social movements in Manipur for political reforms in the State. These popular movements were led by the

Nikhil Manipuri Mahasabha supported by the Assam Congress Committee. The other political organisations supporting the Mahasabha for political reforms were the Manipur Praja Sanmilan, Manipur Krisak Sanmilan, Manipur Youth League, Manipur Mahila Sangha, and Manipur Students' Federation.[81] After the end of the Second World War, the Mahasabha and other groups and parties got themselves amalgamated into the Manipur State Congress (MSC). In the beginning, the Maharaja did not agree to the proposed political reforms and even when he was inclined to introduce the reforms he did not recognise the MSC.[82]

It was in such a political atmosphere that the elections to the Manipur Constitution-making authority were held on January 20, 1947 to elect the five representatives in addition to 10 nominated members—five from the Hill Areas, three from the Darbar, one from Jiribarm area, and one Judge of the Chief Court of Manipur. These fifteen members were to frame the Manipur Constitution Act, 1947. In the elections, the Congress could secure four out of the five elected seats. But the strength of the nominated bloc had weakened their position in the Constitution-making body. However, because of the expected help from the hill areas, the Congress was making an attempt for a coalition in the ministry-making.[83]

This fact was reflected in the conclusions of the three consecutive meetings of the Constitution-making body during March 24–26, 1947. The conclusion 3(iii) specifically stated that one of the features of the "responsive" executive would be: "The representatives to the ultimately elected from the Legislature to form a sort of coalition but with individual responsibility to the legislature".[84] Thus, in this particular feature of the executive in the State we can trace the elements of "responsive", "governmental", and "legislative" coalitions.

After the elections, there were differences of opinion on the formation of the ministry. Ultimately, the Interim Government known as the State Council ministry was formed on August 14, 1947. There were six members in the coalition ministry of the State Council—two each from the MSC, the hill areas, and State officials. The members were Captain Priyabata Singh, Major Khathing, T.C. Tiankham, Krishna Mohan Singh, R.K. Bhuban Singh and Maulabi Basir Uddin Ahmed.[85] But it was not clearly indicated as to who was the Chief Minister. The Maharaja, however, appointed Capt. P.B. Singh, who was nominated from outside the Assembly "to preside over the ministry formed partly by popularly elected members".[86] The Interim Council lasted till October 7, 1948.[87]

On October 8, 1948 a Care-Taker Council was constituted with the same members,[88] and the First Manipur Legislative Assembly under the Manipur Constitution Act, 1947 was inaugurated by the Maharaja.[89] During the Caretaker Council, a number of political developments took place, the most important being the attempts made by the Socialist Party to merge Manipur with Assam; the local Congress Party for the creation of a Purbanchal Pradesh; and the dissident State Congress for the creation of a centrally administered territory. The local Congress Party had the blessings of the Dominion Agent in Manipur, Debeswar Sarma, and the Congress leaders of Assam.[90]

However, both the Governor of Assam and the Chief Minister of Manipur were not at all happy with such developments with certain forces working from outside. Sir Akbar Hydari had even considered Sarma's role as "mischievous", and Gopinath Bordoloi "was taken to task" by Sardar Patel.[91] Ultimately, on November 10, 1948 the new ministry of Manipur State was formed; and in December 1948, Maharaja Kumar P.B. Singh was elected Premier by majority votes.[92] Deb and Lahiri concluded by saying that: "There was a most unexpected coalition of the Praja Party (Pro-Maharaja), the Socialist Party, the Communist Party and All Hill Member who provided a clear majority as opposed to the Congress."[93] Thus, throughout the period of Manipur's semi-independent status (1826), to its protectorate status (1891) and till its State Council status (1947), the strains of coalition politics in various forms and shades had taken place in Manipur.

Manipur, as most of the other Indian Native States, in the end chose to join the Indian Union. After three days of hard negotiation in Shillong, Maharaja Bodh Chandra signed the Instrument of Integration on September 21, 1949.[94] Then, under Articles 239–42, Part IX of the Constitution of India, Manipur became a Part C State to be administered by the Union Government through the Chief Commissioner.

Simultaneously, the Legislative Assembly of Manipur under the Manipur Constitution Act, 1947 was dissolved. In its place, a provision for the Legislature and a Council of Ministers was made under the Part C States (Laws) Act, 1950. Under this Act, Manipur got its new Legislature and nominated Council of Ministers. But their counsels or advices were not binding on the Chief Commissioner.[95] To all intents and purposes, these provisions were meant only to be a transitional arrangement for the smooth transfer of power from a Native State to a State within the Indian Union. This arrangement continued until the First General Elections of 1952, when Manipur had also to elect two members to the Lok Sabha. For this purpose an electoral college of 30 members was constituted.

In the 1952 General Elections for the two Manipur Lok Sabha seats there were as many as 14 political parties which had contested first for the 30-member electoral college. Among these, there were the Congress, Socialist, Communist, All Manipur National Union, Praja Santi, Kuki National Association, Gandhi Sevak Sabha, Historical Research Committee, and Independents. Unlike in 1952, the number of parties contesting the General Elections in 1957 was reduced to four only—Congress, Socialist, Communist, and Praja Socialist besides the Independents.[96] During the 1957 elections instead of an electoral college there was the Territorial Council under the Territorial Councils Act, 1956.[97] The Congress and the Socialist won the Lok Sabha seats with one each in 1952 and 1957 respectively.[98]

The results of the electoral college of 1952 indicated that out of 30 seats no party could secure a majority.

The single largest was, however, the Congress with 10. seats. The other 20 seats went in favour of one Socialist, two Communists, one Gandhi Sevak Sabha, three Praja Santi, three All Manipur National Union, two Kuki National Association, two Mao-Maram Union, one Mizo Union, two Manipur Zeliangroung Union, two Achumba Pamba Congress, and one Independent.[99] In the 1957 elections, the Congress had improved its position in the Territorial Council with 12 members but fell short of a majority. The others were seven Socialists, four Communists, and seven Independents.[100]

The Third General Elections in 1962 while retaining the position of one member each for the Congress and the Socialist in the Lok Sabha, in the Territorial Council, the Congress had half (15) of the members which was short of a majority. The Socialist won five seats and 10 Independents.[101] On August 3, 1963 the Territorial Council was upgraded to the status of the Legislative Assembly preceding by a popular government under the Chief Ministership of Mairembam Koireng Singh of the Congress on July 1, 1963.[102] The principle of a coalition ministry did not figure out prominently at that time as the Congress had already secured half of the total seats But since the help of the Independents was very much there, it may still be called a Congress-led coalition government.[103]

It was in the Fourth General Elections of 1967 that the election results had undergone a significant change. For the Lok Sabha seats both the Congress and the Socialists were defeated, and the seats went one each to the Communist and the Independent.[104] But in the Legislative Assembly, the Congress secured an absolute majority with 16 seats while the Samyukta Socialist Party (SSP) secured four, one CPI, and nine Independents.[105] In the mid-term poll for the Lok Sabha Elections of 1971, the Congress fortune had improved further when it captured both the seats.[106]

At this stage, it would be very interesting to observe the fluctuations in the political scenario of Manipur which process had started the political instability in the State.

After the 1967 elections, the Congress with 16 members formed the government. It had increased its strength to 23 when seven Independents joined its camp. However, in October 1967, the Congress was reduced to a minority when nine members defected and the Koireng Singh ministry had to resign. After his resignation, the first formal coalition government in the State was formed under the name and style of the United Front Government under the leadership of Longjam Thambou Singh, a defected member from the Congress. Later on, the Speaker resigned and the Congress had the equal strength of members. As a result, a political deadlock ensued when no side was willing to stake the claim for Speakership. Thambou Singh was forced to resign after 12 days only in office. The Assembly had, therefore, to be suspended from October 1967 to February 1968 when the State was placed under the President's Rule.[107]

With the regrouping of members during the President's Rule, the Congress could claim a majority when six more members joined its Party, though one of them was unseated later on. The Congress ministry was formed on February 19, 1968. At this juncture, it may be noted that the 30-member Territorial Assembly was increased to 32 with the nominated members till March 1969, which was later on increased to 33 with one more nominated member. So, in March 1969, the Congress had 22 members in a 33-member House. But on September 10, 1969 12 Congressmen resigned from the party and formed a United Legislature Party (ULP) under the leadership of Md. Alimuddin supported by four SSP, one CPI and three Independents. While the membership of the SSP and the CPI remained intact throughout this period, the constant defections from the Congress and Independents made it impossible for the formation of a viable coalition government or otherwise. As a result, the government of India had to impose another President's Rule from October 1969 till the Fifth General Elections in March 1972.[108]

The full-fledged State of Manipur was inaugurated on February 1, 1972. With the new status of the State, the strength of the Legislative Assembly was also raised from

33 to 60.[109] Immediately after its inauguration as a new State of the Indian Union, Manipur went to the Fifth General Elections alongwith the rest of the country in March 1972. This election marked a great departure from the previous elections in the State in the sense that there was a complete break down of the one-party domi nance. No single party could secure even 1/3 of the seats. While the Congress secured 17 seats, Socialist—three, CPI—five, Congress (O)—1, Manipur People's Party (MPP)—15, and 19 Independents.[110] The Independents included the unrecognised parties like the United Naga Integration Council (UNIC)—with three seats. The large number of Independents has been almost a regular feature in Manipur. It was in such a situation that a coalition government becomes inevitable.

In the beginning, the Congress was toying with the idea of forming a government. But later on it decided to sit in the opposition. The MPP with 15 members then along with three Socialists, three Congress (O), 10 Independents and one Congress defector formed the United Legislature Party (ULP) with 32 members under the leadership of Md. Alimuddin.[111] The new coalition ministry was sworn-in on March 20, 1972. The days later, the ULP strength increased from 32 to 35 on March 30, 1972;[112] and settled with 36 members on May 25, 1972.[113] In July 1972, three UNIC members (Independents) left the ULP to join the Congress, but the ULP survived with 33 members.[114] In November 1972, the ULP again increased its strength with 36 members. It is clearly a case of engineering defections on both sides — the ruling and the opposition.

The House lost one member of the ruling coalition when he passed away on March 10, 1973. On March 15, 1973 nine ULP members formed themselves a Progressive Independent Group and joined the opposition to form the Progressive Democratic Alliance (PDA) under the leadership of Atikho Daiho of the Congress.[115] Clearly, Alimuddin with 26 members only was in the minority and had to resign on March 26, 1973 amidst the battle of defections and no-confidence motion. The Chief

Minister, Alimuddin while giving his report to the Governor observed that "two defectors had the record of changing sides four times each and both of them were Congressmen, while some Congress members defected thrice" and further opined that: "In the counter-defections the support by some defectors to any ministry is bound to be extremely fake and unreal".[116] The Governor while forwarding the note of the Chief Minister agreed in his report that: "It is true that in a legislature in which 18 members have changed sides within a period of one year there is no certainty that any government will be stable".[117] The end result was that the third President's Rule was imposed in Manipur and the Legislative Assembly was dissolved on March 28, 1973.

In early 1974 the mid-term poll to the State Assembly was held where five national parties—Congress, Congress (O), Socialist, CPI and CPI (M); and three regional parties—MPP, Manipur Hills Union (MHU), and Kuki National Assembly (KNA) in addition to a large number of Independents took part. There was a pre-poll alliance or coalition between the Congress and the CPI on one hand and the MPP and the MHU on the other.[118]

The results of the elections did not bring out any majority party. The Congress secured 12 seats, Socialist —two, CPI—six, MPP—20, MHU—11, KNA—two, and seven Independents. The "era of coalitions and counter-coalitions" had come into existence observed R.P. Singh. The first coalition after the 1974 elections led by Alimuddin of the ULP was formed on March 4, 1974 but lasted only for four months.[119] The next coalition ministry was headed by Yangmaso Shaiza of the Progressive Democratic Front (PDF) on July 10, 1974 which existed for about five months. On December 6, 1974 the third coalition government of Democratic Legislature Party (DLP) was formed with R.K. Dorendra Singh as the leader. This coalition remained in power for about eight months. After three consecutive coalitions had failed to bring in political stability in the State, the Congress took over the reins of power on July 23, 1975 with R.K. Dorendra Singh as its leader. This government continued during the period of the National Emergency in the country. Before the end of the Emergency, the Sixth Lok Sabha Elections 1977 were held and the Congress captured both the Manipur seats.[120]

After the Lok Sabha poll of 1977 which brought about the first non-Congress coalition Janata ministry at the Centre, the whole Congress Legislature Party of Manipur defected to Janata and formed the first Janata government in Manipur with Yangmaso Shaiza, M.P., as its leader. But with the split of the Janata at the Centre, the Janata Party in Manipur also went out and the Legislative Assembly was dissolved on November 14, 1979.[121]

The General Elections of January 1980 that followed were for both the Lok Sabha and the State Assembly. For the Lok Sabha the two seats went in favour of Congress (I) and CPI with one seat each.[122] In the Assembly Elections during the same period, the same result came out in which no party could gain a majority.[123]

Congress (I)	13	MPP :	4	
Janata :	10	KNA :	2	
Congress (U):	6	Independents :	19	
CPI :	5			
		Total :	59	(one seat yet to go for the poll).

This result brought again into existence another spell of a coalition government of the Congress(I), Congress(U), MPP and most of the Independents. Dorendra Singh was sworn-in as the Chief Minister of this new coalition on January 17, 1980. But, sometime later, the Manipur National Democratic Party (MNDP) formed by some members who had defected from their respective parties merged themselves with the MPP. This had resulted again in the instability of Dorendra Singh's ministry, and could not complete the term.[124]

Political instability has been the unique feature of Manipur politics. But after the assassination of Indira Gandhi in October 1984, the sympathy wave for the Congress(I) had swept the whole country. Manipur was no exception. That was why in the General Elections to the State Assembly on December 24 and 27, 1984 the Congress(I) secured 30 seats, while the MPP secured three, Janata—four, KNA and CPI with one each, and 21 Independents. Later on, the Congress(I) gained the majority by admitting four Independents. It was the single party majority government led by Rishang Keishing who was sworn-in on January 3, 1985.[125] But the fact that the Independents had come to the rescue of the Congress(I) in the formation and continuation of the stability of the Government, it can safely be concluded that it is not entirely a single party government. The element of coalition politics persisted which had later on caused political instability in the State.

But the major period of political instability in Manipur was after the General Elections which were held on February 12, 1990. The party position of the elections was:[126]

Congress (I)	26	CPI	3	
Janata Dal	10	KNA	2	
MPP	10	National People's Party (NPP)	1	
Indian Congress Socialist (Congress–S)	6	Total	58	(Later on JD and MPP got one each making a total of 60).

The 1990 Elections did not produce any single party commanding a majority in the House. The Congress(I) being the single largest party could have made an attempt to form the ministry. But the incumbency factor during the previous regime made in difficult for the party to get the support of other parties. As a result the United Legislature Front (ULF) formed the coalition ministry. The new ministry was led by R.K. Ranbir Singh (MPP) as Chief Minister and Phumujam Amutombi Singh (JD) as Deputy Chief Minister who assumed office on February 23, 1990.[127]

The ULF ministry was a six-party coalition. The other Ministers were L. Ibomcha Singh (Congress–S), T.N.

Haokip (KNA), V. Hangkhaliam (NPP) as Minister of State, and one CPI Minister. The ULF coalition ministry worked with a "common programme" like the demand for the inclusion of the Manipuri Language in the Eighth Schedule to the Constitution of India. However, the ULF coalition could not provide a stable government due to internal bickerings. Such internal bickerings took place even in the United Opposition Front.[128] The result of such internal bickerings on both sides had enabled the Congress (I) to take over power for sometime with R.K. Dorendra Singh as Chief Minister. But the Congress (I)-led coalition also could not survive due to ethnic violence in the State. This led to the imposition of President's Rule in the State on December 31, 1993.

The President's Rule continued for 346 days. It ended on December 12, 1994. On December 13, 1994 Rishang Keishing replaced R.K. Dorendra Singh as Chief Minister. This new ministry was also a Congress (I)-led coalition. But because of a change of guard, the four Congress(S) —Chongkokai Dongel, Holkhomang Haokip, Bajra Gopal Singh, and R.N. Ibomcha SIngh withdrew their support for Keishing.[129] The Keishing coalition ministry could survive because the Speaker, Dr. H. Borababu Singh was removed and replaced by W. Angou as Pro-term Speaker. Borababu Singh was removed because he had expelled 23 members in order to defeat the coalition ministry. But the High Court passed an order staying the expulsion of the 23 members. Borababu SIngh through a Special Leave Petition appealed to the Supreme Court to set aside the High Court's order and the 23 members could attend the Assembly.[130]

After 28 days, a no-confidence motion was tabled against the Keishing's coalition ministry. But it was defeated by 37 to 21 votes. The Congress (I)-led coalition would have eroded further. But because the term of the ministry would be only upto the February General Elections, it could continue to complete its term.

In the next General Elections which were held on February 16 and 19, 1995 the results again indicated the trend towards an era of coalition politics in Manipur. The results were as follow:[131]

Congress (I)	: 22	NPP	: 2
MPP	: 18	Samajwdi Party	: 2
JD	: 7	BJP	: 1
CPI	: 2	Congress(S)	: 1
Federal Party of Manipur (FPM)	: 2	Independents	: 3
		Total	: 60

The Congress Party being the single largest party had an edge over the MPP. The Joint Legislature Party (JLP) was formed and a coalition ministry under Rishang Keishing (Congress) as Chief Minister was installed on February 25, 1995. The position of the ruling and opposition parties was as follows:[132]

Ruling JLP		Opposition United Legislature Front (ULF)	
Congress	: 22	MPP	: 18
Progressive JD	: 4	CPI	: 2
NPP	: 2	JD	: 2
Samata Party	: 2		
		Total	: 22
JD (Sehpu Group)	: 1		
Congress (S)	: 1		
Independents	: 3		
Total	: 37		

The lone BJP member did not support either side. It should be noted that there had been defections/splits and renaming of parties and groups after the elections.

Meanwhile, three was an erosion of support to the JLP when 10 members including Progressive JD, NPP, Samata Party, Federal Party, JD (Sehpu Group), and one Independent formed another opposition front called the United Democratic Front (UDF).[133] Accordingly, the no-confidence motion was brought against the Keishing coalition ministry on July 31, 1995. The Speaker, W. Nipamacha Singh disqualified five opposition members to give Keishing 27 against 26 opposition. But even after disqualifying the five members, the House was tied up with 27 to 27. The Speaker would have to exercise his casting vote had it not been for the lone BJP member who had saved the JLP coalition by abstaining from voting.[134]

The result was so disappointing to the opposition that the two fronts (ULF and UDF) had to combine themselves together on September 5, 1995 with MPP (18), CPI and JD one each of the ULF on the one side, and the Federal Party (2), and Samata Party (1) of the UDF on the other side bringing in a total of 23 members only. The case of the other five members who had been disqualified was then pending in the Supreme Court. Thus, even with this new combination, the JLP coalition had still a majority of 32 members.[135]

It was only on November 23, 1995 that another no-confidence motion was moved against the Keishing coalition ministry. The motion was defeated by a bigger margin of 37 against and only 16 for the motion. The JLP coalition of Keishing had increased its strength from 32 to 37 with the defection of some members from the MPP(K) a splinter group of the MPP.[136]

But the Keishing coalition ministry lasted for only 35 months. When a member of dissidents from the Congress(I) withdrew their support, Keishing found himself to be in a minority. The House was summoned on December 15, 1997 for a vote of confidence. The motion was lost by 17 (16 Congress and one Independent) to 38 (23 renegade Congress and 15 from MPP, FPM, CPI and two Independent). The House at that time consisted of 55 members (four disqualified and one was killed by extremists in November 1997). When Keishing was voted out, the four-party coalition called the United Front formed a coalition ministry with Wahengbam Nipamacha (MSC, a splinter group of Congress) as Chief Minister along with other Ministers from MSC, and three from MPP. The other two coalition partners were the FPM and the CPI.[137] Nipamacha continues to be the Chief Minister of the UF coalition till the time of writing.

Till today no one can really know for sure which way the ruling and opposition members in the Manipur Assembly would behave. It is perhaps the only State in North-East India where political instability is the rule rather than an exception. This kind of political behaviour on the part of the elected representatives of Manipur indicates the political configuration of the State—the hill politics versus the valley politics as well as the ethnic politics both in the hill areas and in the valley. The strategic position of the State in the periphery of a big country from the point of view of the insurgency movements, and the sense of *irredentism* on the part of the people of the State are also contributing factors to continuing political instability in the foreseeable future. Because of this kind of political instability, Manipur would continue the process of coalition politics of ministry-making and ministry-breaking only to be punctuated occasionally by President's Rule. We are only awaiting for the next General Elections in the State around 2000 A.D., if not earlier, and see if the process of coalition politics in the State can be reversed.

MEGHALAYA

The area of present day Meghalaya was a part of Assam and consisted of its two districts of Garo Hills, and the United Khasi—Jaintia Hills. It had its first taste of coalition politics when it was a part of Assam both during the colonial regime when Rev. J.J.M. Nichols-Roy participated in the various coalitions of that period (1920–46); and during the composite State of Assam when the EITU members joined the Chaliha ministry. Captain W.A. Sangma, the EITU leader, joined the Congress-led coalition on May 27, 1958 as Cabinet Minister followed by Larsingh Khyriem as Deputy Minister. But this coalition lasted only for a period of two and a half years.[138]

As observed earlier in the section on Assam in Part II this coalition was as a matter of political expediency only. The decision of the EITU itself was not unanimous. There were two divergent views but ultimately EITU "decided the proposal by a majority vote" simply to honour the wishes of the Prime Minister and not for a genuine desire for such a coalition. Therefore, it was only a question of time before the coalition could be ended. The opportunity for such an ending came when the Government of Assam went ahead with the implementation of its Assamese Language Policy. This led to the resignation of all the EITU members of the Chaliha coalition ministry in October 1960.[139]

For about 10 years the elected representatives from Meghalaya area were either sitting in the opposition or boycotting the Assembly Elections. It was only in 1969 that the Assam Reorganisation (Meghalaya) Act was passed in the Parliament. According to the provisions of this Act, the Autonomous State of Meghalaya within Assam was created. The Act made a further provision for an elected representative to the Assam Legislative Assembly from the Autonomous State of Meghalaya which was not filled up. Another provision was that there was to be a provisional Legislative Assembly also with 38 elected and three nominated members. The electors for the Provisional Assembly were the members of the three Autonomous District Councils as electoral colleges for the representatives to be elected from the areas falling within their respective district council. The elections were held in March 1970 with 16 seats from Garo Hills, 18 from Khasi Hills, and four from Jaintia Hills.[140] The results of the elections were in favour of the APHLC Excepting for the four Congress members from Garo Hills, all the 34 members belonged to the APHLC. Even the three nominated members also joined the APHLC. In fact, the four Congress members too had aligned themselves with the APHLC. This was so because it was at the initiative of Capt. Sangma that a pre-poll alliance was made in Garo Hills area between the APHLC with 12 seats and the Congress with four seats.[141] In Khasi and Jaintia Hills there was no such pre-poll alliance where it was entirely an APHLC affair. Only in Jaintia Hills there was a lone non-APHLC lady candidate contesting for one of the four seats allotted to that district council; and the candidate lost the election.

Naturally, the ministry of the Provincial Legislative Assembly of Meghalaya was the APHLC ministry with Capt. Sangma as the Chief Minister. But because of the alliance of the Congress with the APHLC even in the House, the Sangma ministry may be called as an APHLC-led coalition. And because of the "electoral adjustment" the post of Deputy Speaker was given to the Congress, notwithstanding the parliamentary practice.[142] To sum up, the ministry of the Meghalaya Provisional Legislative Assembly was a grand coalition where there was no opposition party at all. Meanwhile, the Autonomous State of Meghalaya was upgraded into a full-fledged Statehood, separately from Assam, with a Legislative Assembly of its own under the North-Eastern Areas (Reorganisation) Act, 1971. The First General Elections to the new 60-member Meghalaya Legislative Assembly was held on March 9, 1972. This time there were pre-poll alliances between the APHLC and the Congress in Garo Hills—18 APHLC and six Congress;[143] and in Khasi Hills—25 APHLC and four Congress.[144] Strangely, there was no such pre-poll alliance in Jaintia Hills and the six seats were a free for all where the Congress fought against the APHLC candidates.[145] The results of the elections were again in favour of the APHLC with 39 seats followed by Congress with 11 seats, and the other 10 seats went to the Independents (including eight seats for the then unrecognised party of the Hill State People's Democratic Party or HSPDP).[146]

But in spite of the pre-poll alliances in the two districts, unlike in the Provisional Assembly (1970), there was no post-poll alliance after the elections and the ministry was formed by the APHLC all by itself, But because of the pre-poll alliance, there was such an understanding between the APHLC and the Congress including the two independents. Only the HSPDP was the main opposition party. Technically, therefore, it may be said that in spite of the single party ministry of the APHLC, there was a legislative coalition between the APHLC and the Congress.

Gradually, this understanding at the legislative level led to the break-up of the APHLC at the Mendipathar (Garo Hills) Conference of the APHLC on November 16, 1976. When the APHLC group led by Capt. Sangma merged itself with the Congress and formed the single party ministry of the Congress for the first time in

Meghalaya on November 22, 1976.[147] The other APHLC group led by B.B. Lyngdoh had to sit, like the HSPDP, in the opposition. Of course, some HSPDP members also had defected to the Congress camp along with the Capt. Sangma APHLC group. This took place at a time when there was the Congress split at the Centre. In the confused state of the Congress split at the Centre, Capt. Sangma's Congress group was for sometime aligning itself with the Congress (B) of Brahmana Reddy, though later on switched over its allegiance to the Congress(I) group. It was during that time that there was an intra-party coalition in the State Congress camp—the Capt. Sangma group and the Nina Rynjah group.

However, the first real coalition ministry in Meghalaya was the one experimented after the February 25, 1978 General Elections to the Second Assembly. The results of the elections were:[148] Congress—20, APHLC—16, HSPDP—14, and 10 Independents (including two from the then unrecognised party, the Public Demands Implementation Convention or PDIC). Since no party could obtain a majority in the House, a coalition ministry was inevitable. But it took more than a week for the regional parties to come to an understanding to form a coalition ministry. A series of discussions were held during March 3–7, 1978 but there was a complete deadlock on the issue of the leadership of the proposed coalition.

It was at this juncture that the Meghalaya Tribal Youth Organisation demanded that the leaders of the regional parties should settle the issue of leadership and form the non-Congress government. The issue of leadership was finally settled by drawing of lots on the midnight of March 9, 1978. On March 10, 1978 the Meghalaya United Legislative Party (MULP) coalition ministry was sworn in with D.D. Pugh (APHLC) as Chief Minister and S.D. Khongwir (HSPDP) as Deputy Chief Minister. The other coalition partner was the PDIC. As it was a three-party coalition it was popularly called the "Three-Flag Government" and the opposition under the Congress-led coalition, the Meghalaya United Legislature Front (MULF) branded the MULP coalition government as the "Lottery Government".

The MULP coalition government being a forced marriage could not last for long. On February 21, 1979 the HSPDP partners were thrown out, and the "Two-Flag" coalition government of the APHLC and the PDIC was sworn in with D.D. Pugh (APHLC) as the Chief Minister.[149]

The Chief Minister preferred to call his government as the APHLC government just to satisfy his party men, though in fact it was a coalition with the PDIC. The action of D.D. Pugh, however, caused a split in the APHLC camp. The veteran APHLC leader B.B. Lyngdoh and his colleague S.D.D. Nichols-Roy did not even attend the swearing-in ceremony.[150] It was a clear indication that the downfall of the "Two-Flag" coalition government was a matter of time only. An ultimatum was issued by B.B. Lyngdoh on March 23, 1978 to D.D. Pugh to immediately break away from an alliance with the PDIC which was not complied with by the latter.[151]

It was at this critical juncture that the HSPDP had egged on B.B. Lyngdoh (APHLC) and Capt. Sangma (Congress) to join together and overthrow the Pugh's coalition ministry. The three parties accordingly formed the United Meghalaya Parliamentary Democratic Forum (UMPDF) on April 17, 1978 under the leadership of B.B. Lyngdoh (APHLC) and entered into a "solemn, serious agreement" and "to form a sort of national government .... federal in form that will always ensure a stable majority in the Assembly".[152]

This was followed by a vote of confidence in the Pugh's coalition ministry on May 4, 1979. The situation in the House was so tense that there was not even an objection to the motion nor was there any discussion too. The Speaker had simply to put the motion for voting which was defeated by 30 to 29 votes. On May 17, 1978 the UMPDF coalition ministry was formed with B.B. Lyngdoh (APHLC) as Chief Minister for two years only. The "solemn, serious agreement" also provided that after two years, Capt. Sangma (Congress) would take over as the next Chief Minister of the UMPDF coalition for the next two years. The "solemn, serious agreement" was honoured by all the UMPDF partners, including the HSPDP which would continue to hold the post of Deputy Chief Minister for four years, till the next General Elections in 1983.[153] Thus Meghalaya had the distinction of having a lottery government among the coalition partners, and a 50 : 50 sharing of power in the coalition government during the tenure of the Second Assembly.

The Third General Elections to the Meghalaya Legislative Assembly were held on February 17, 1983. This time again, no party could obtain a majority in the House. The results were:[154] Congress(I)—25, APHLC—15, HSPDP —15, PDIC—2, and three Independents. The three regional parties with a total of 34 members—APHLC now with 17 members, HSPDP—15, and PDIC—2 formed the Meghalaya United Parliamentary Party (MUPP). But the leadership issue was the main bone of contention. Ultimately, B.B. Lyngdoh (APHLC) became the Chief Minister and H.S. Lyngdoh (HSPDP) the Deputy Chief Minister. The new MUPP coalition ministry was sworn in on March 2, 1983. But because of dissidence and defections within its camp, the MUPP lasted only for 29 days.[155]

Taking advantage of the MUPP's weakness, the Congress (I) moved a no-confidence motion on March 31, 1983. The motion was carried by 31 votes to 27, while one member, D.R. Nongkynrih of the MUPP coalition ministry remained absent at the time of voting. After the fall of the MUPP coalition ministry, another coalition ministry called the Meghalaya Democratic Front (MDF) under the leadership of Capt. Sangma (Congress) took over power on April 2, 1983. The MDF coalition government, which was a Congress dominated government, continued till the 1988 General Elections.

Before the 1988 General Elections to the State Assembly, there was the 1984 General Elections to the Lok Sabha. With the announcement for the 1984 elections, and five weeks before the polling, the regional opposition parties made an attempt for an opposition coalition or alliance. Both the APHLC and the HSPDP after prolonged discussions came to the decision to unite the two parties under the banner of the Hill People Union (HPU) on November 16, 1984. The HPU after being defeated in the Lok Sabha polls again became a divided house with the HSPDP claiming a separate existence. Similarly, there was another faction of the dissolved APHLC which claimed a separate existence of the APHLC which was later on recognised by the Election Commission as the APHLC (A) with Armison Marak as its leader.

The 1988 General Elections to the Fourth Assembly held on February 2, 1988 were contested under the above changing political situations. With the regional parties (opposition) in political disarray, the Congress (I) as the ruling party under the MDF coalition had expected to reap a rich dividend. But it proved to be the continuation of another spell of coalition governments in the State. The results of the 1988 elections were:[156]

Congress (I)	: 21	APHLC (A)	: 2
HPU	: 19	Independents	: 9
HSPDP	: 5	Results withheld	: 2
PDIC	: 2	Total	: 60

(later on, one seat went to the Congress (I) making a total of 22).

The regional parties could have managed to form a coalition. But again because of disunity, defections, and differences in the opposition camp, the Congress (I) as the single largest party could capture power and was able to lead the United Meghalaya Parliamentary Forum (UMPF) with Purno A. Sangma (Congress) as Chief Minister, and D.D. Lapang (Congress) as Deputy Chief Minister. B.B. Lyngdoh (HPU) was appointed Chairman of the State Planning Board with a Cabinet rank.

The UMPF was a three-party coalition—Congress (I) —22, HPU (BB)—7, APHLC (A)—2, and Independents—4 making a total of 35 members in the House of 59. The opposition coalition party was known as the Regional Democratic Front (RDF) led by S.D. Khongwir (HPU) with HPU—12, HSPDP—5, PDIC—2, and Independents—5 totaling 24 in all. A no-confidence motion was moved on

February 25, 1988 by the opposition RDF coalition but was defeated by the ruling UMPF coalition.[157]

In early 1990, the Congress (I)-led UMPF coalition was reduced to a minority because half of its members deserted it. The split in the UMPF had enabled the dissident group to join hands with the regional parties and formed the Meghalaya United Parliamentary Party (MUPP) coalition with B.B. Lyngdoh (APHLC—B) as Chief Minister. But there was a difference of opinion between the Governor and the Speaker over the status of one Congress (I) member, H.B. Dan. The Speaker had given a ruling that there was a split in the UMPF and the shifting of alliance of H.B. Dan to MUPP was recognised. But the Governor doubted the Speaker's contention as the Congress (I) had objected to Dan's inclusion in the MUPP. When the matter was referred by the Governor to the State Attorney General, the MUPP criticised the Governor's "partisan role" and threatened that he should be removed and a new Governor should replace him. At this juncture, the Governor administered the oaths of office and secrecy on May 22, 1990.[158]

This action of the Governor had brought about another controversy raised by the Congress (I). Meanwhile, there were also dissident groups in both camps, making the MUPP coalition ministry unstable. The MUPP was in a precarious position when in a trial of strength in the House, the Speaker had disqualified five members, thereby turning the MUPP into a minority. The President's Rule was then imposed in Meghalaya on October 12, 1991.[159] The MUPP then challenged in the Court of Law on the action of the Speaker and the imposition of President's Rule. The contention of the MUPP was that their coalition ministry was still a majority when the coalition government was removed from power. While the Court case went on, the Congress (I) could prove its majority of 32 members and was called upon to assume power on the revocation of the President's Rule. The Congress (I)-led UMPF coalition government was led by D.D. Lapang as Chief Minister and J.D. Pohrmen as Deputy Chief Minister. P.A. Sangma by then had been elected to the

Lok Sabha during the 1991 General Elections. The second UMPF coalition government was sworn-in on February 6, 1992.[160] Later on, the Supreme Court decided the case in favour of the MUPP. But by that time another coalition ministry had already been sworn in after the 1993 General Elections to the Fifth Assembly.

During the 1993 General Elections, Meghalaya once again could not return any majority party to the State Assembly. The results were as follows:[161]

Congress (I)	: 24	PDIC	: 2
HPU	: 11	Meghalaya Progressive People's Party	: 2
HSPDP	: 8		
APHLC (A)	: 3	Independents	: 10
Total	: 60		

A coalition ministry led by the Congress (I) under Salseng C. Marak took the oath of office and secrecy with the help of the split in the HSPDP (L) and APHLC (A) as well as the support of some Independents. Inspite of a small margin of majority in the initial stages, this coalition which was called the Meghalaya United Front (MUF) could complete its term in office. This was the only government which could complete its full term in the 25 years long history of the Meghalaya Legislative Assembly.

The last General Elections to the Sixth Assembly were held on February 16, 1998. This election had again produced no majority party. The united opposition among the three regional parties, the HPU, PDIC and a section of the HSPDP under its President, E.K. Mawlong formed the United Democratic Party (UDP) just on the eve of the elections and expected to achieve a better performance because of the unity in the regional camp. However, the HSPDP leader as usual refused to join the UDP unity formation of the regional parties. Naturally, the opposition was again a disunited group with the Garo National Council (GNC) of Garo Hills splitting from the HPU under the leadership of Clifford Marak. Only in Jaintia Hills, for the first time in its political history that the opposition party (UDP) had captured all the seven seats, which was a 100 per cent success. Another feature of the elections was that the BJP had for the first time opened its account, though earlier there was an Independent who joined it. The results of the elections were as follows:[162]

Congress (I)	: 25	Public Democratic Movement (PDM)	: 3
UDP	: 20	GNC	: 1
BJP	: 3	Independents	: 5
HSPDP	: 3	Total	: 60

The Congress (I) as the single largest party had staked its claim for forming the government, and Salseng C. Marak formed the Congress (I)—led government on February 27, 1998. But it was the government with the shortest tenure of 12 days only, as it could not muster an absolute majority. During the process of government formation, it claimed to have a coalition majority of 36 members with three each of the HSPDP, PDM, and five Independents. But after the defeat of its candidate for the office of Speakership the "coalition" ministry of S.C. Marak resigned without facing a trust vote.

The second coalition ministry in the Sixth Assembly called the United Democratic Front (UDF) under the leadership of B.B. Lyngdoh (UDP) then assumed office on March 10, 1998 along with 20 UDP, three BJP, three HSPDP, one GNC and four Independents.[163] But immediately after the swearing-in there were claims and counter claims from both the ruling UDF coalition under the leadership of the UDP and the opposition coalition under the leadership of the Congress (I). This led to defection and redefection of two HSPDP members which had caused a split in the HSPDP. The split had further caused the instability of the UDF coalition ministry.

There was also an indication of a split in the UDP itself which was a major partner in the UDF coalition. The Congress (I) could clearly see the possibility of leading another coalition ministry in the event of the collapse of the UDF coalition. It was in such a situation that B.B. Lyngdoh, the Chief Minister of the UDF coalition resigned on July 27, 1998; and the same day a new

UDP-Congress (I) coalition called the Meghalaya Parliamentary Forum (MPF) was installed with B.B. Lyngdoh (UDP) as Chief Minister and D.D. Lapang (Congress-I) as Deputy Chief Minister on a 50: 50 basis of power sharing in the coalition of a duration of about two years each. It is yet to be seen whether this agreement between the regional party and the national party would-be as solemn and serious as in the 1979 coalition ministry. Thus, within five months after the February 1998 General Elections there were three coalition ministries in the State of Meghalaya.

The 1998 General Elections in Meghalaya had produced the following special features:

1. The Congress (I)-led "coalition" ministry of Salseng C. Marak with the tenure of 12 days only which was the shortest so far in the 25-year history of Meghalaya;
2. The formation of three coalitions within a period of exactly five months only from February 27, 1998 to July 27, 1998, again the highest number so far in the 25-year history of Meghalaya; and
3. The over-sized MPF coalition ministry on "political compulsion" with 35 Ministers including the Chief Minister in the House of 60 members, which was again the biggest ever in the 25-year history of Meghalaya.

Perhaps, Meghalaya is the only State in India, if not in the whole world, which has the unique distinction of continuously having coalition governments for over 25 years ever since its inception; a coalition government by drawing of lots; a 50 : 50 basis of power sharing in the coalition government not only once but now for a second time; a coalition ministry of more than 58 per cent of the total membership of the House on "political compulsion"; invariably all the 60 members of the House becoming Ministers by turn in a term of five years; legislature parties with no concrete ideology; three coalition governments within a period of five months; one coalition government completing its full term of five years;

and the dismissal of one coalition government having a majority in the House. It is yet to be seen how many times of these salient features will be repeated until the next General Elections in 2003 and in future as well.

MIZORAM

The major British contact with Mizoram was with the Lushai Expeditions of 1871–72 and 1886–89.[164] The expeditions resulted in the annexation of Lushai Hills. In the beginning the area was divided into two parts—the Northern Lushal Hills under the administrative control of the Chief Commissioner of Assam, and the Southern Lushai Hills under the Lieutenant Governor of Bengal. It was only in the Chin-Lushai Conference of 1898 that the two parts were combined into one administrative unit under the administrative control of the Chief Commissioner of Assam. The combined area was then called the Lushai Hills district of Assam incharge of the Superintendent instead of a Deputy Commissioner.[165]

Before India's independence, the Lushai Hills district was not represented in any legislature, Central or Provincial. Under the Government of India Act, 1919 it was declared a backward area, and under the Government of India Act, 1935 it was placed under the Excluded Area. As a result, till independence there was no representation nor nomination of legislators from Lushai Hills neither in the Legislative Council nor the Legislative Assembly of Assam.[166] The laws for the district were enacted by the Executive corresponding to the Order-in-Council by the British Crown through the Governor of Assam as the Crown representative acting as the Agent to the Governor-General of India. In fact, the British did not interfere much with the traditional administrative institutions of the Chiefs in Lushai Hills.

However, when India's independence was approaching, the Superintendent of Lushai Hills, Major A. Macdonald prepared a scheme in 1941 for the District Conference where there was an equal representation of 20 members each for the Chiefs and the Commoners respectively. All the 350 Chiefs would be an electoral college for electing the 20 Chiefs as members of the District Conference, and 2510 voters (on the basis of a group of 10 houses in the village as a unit) as another electoral college for electing the 20 commoners to the District Conference. So, for the first time in the history of Mizoram, the system of election was introduced in Lushai Hills. The First District Conference was held in January 1946, and the Second District Conference in 1947. But in the 1947 elections, instead of a separate electorate, there was a joint electorate with two ballots for each voter (one for electing a Chief and another for electing a Commoner). It was definitely an improvement on the electoral process in Lushai Hills.[167]

Meanwhile, the Bordoloi Committee for Assam Tribal and Excluded Areas of the Constituent Assembly had made recommendations for the inclusion of Lushai Hills under the Sixth Schedule to the Constitution of India. The Constituent Assembly accepted the recommendation and made a provision for an Autonomous District Council for Lushai Hills and also for an Autonomous Regional Council for the Pawi-Lakher region of Lushai Hills district.[168] The Autonomous District Council and the Regional Council for the Lushai Hills district were established only in 1952 under the Constitution of India, 1950. Besides the district and regional councils, Lushai Hills was also allotted three seats in the Assam Legislative Assembly. The district and regional councils had both elected and nominated members while the three seats in the Assembly were all elective.[169]

Earlier, from August 15, 1947 the administration of Lushai Hills was carried on through the traditional institutions of the village councils of the Chiefs and the District Conference; and from 1950 through the village councils of the Chiefs and the Tribal Advisory Council acting as a Provisional Autonomous District Council until the General Elections of 1952. The traditional institution of Chiefship was abolished in 1954 and the Lushai Hills district was renamed the Mizo Hills district.[170] Thus, from India's independence till 1952 the Lushai Hills district was not represented in the Assam Legislative Assembly until the First General Elections of 1952.

Then, from 1952 to 1972 the Mizo Hills district was represented in the Assam Assembly by the Mizo Union (MU) party. Only when the MU was part of the EITU that it had participated in the Congress-led coalition ministry of Assam during 1958–60 with Lalmawia as Minister of State and A. Thanglura as the Chief Parliamentary Secretary. But, A. Thanglura from Mizo Hills refused to resign along with the other EITU Ministers in 1960. Instead, he shifted his allegiance to the Congress Party. In any case, the first experience of Mizo Hills in coalition politics was during that time.[171]

A study of the electoral politics in Mizoram would indicate that excepting during the first ministry after the First General Elections of 1972 when the Union Territory of Mizoram went to the polls, and during the Mizoram Peace Accord of 1986 when coalition politics was experimented between the Mizo National Front (MNF) and the Congress, the Union Territory was free from coalition politics at the inter-party level. There were of course intra-party coalitions as among the Mizo Union Council of MU (of Pachhunga and R. Vanlawma) and the Mizo Union Right Wing of MU of Lalsawia;[172] the two Congress factions of Dengthuama and Hrangchuama;[173] People's Conference (A) of Chief Minister Brigadier T. Sailo and People's Conference (B) of Thangridema;[174] and MNF (Laldenga) and MNF (Democratic) of Chawngzuala.[175]

It was only by 1972 when the Union Territories (Amendment Act), 1971 was passed that the Mizo Hills district was upgraded into the status of a Union Territory of Mizoram. The Union Territory had a Legislative Assembly consisting of 30 elected and three nominated members. When the Union Territory was upgraded into a full-fledged State of Mizoram in 1987 the strength of the Legislative Assembly was raised to 40 seats.

In the First General Elections of 1972 the Mizo Union captured 21 seats in the House of 30. The Congress secured six and three Independents. It was rather strange that after winning the elections, no one from the Congress would be willing to be the first Chief Minister. Sprawnga and Chhunga, the two senior leaders of the Congress, both tried to shift the responsibility to each other. In the end Sprawnga could persuade Chhunga to take up the responsibility, and formed the MU ministry in May 1972. But on May 3, 1974 a merger between the MU and the Congress took place and in addition to five MU Ministers, two Congress members were made Ministers in the Chhunga ministry.[176] There may be a difference between a merger and a coalition, but the fact that the two parties coalesced or merged with each other it is a case of a coalition politics.

The Second General Elections in 1978 gave an absolute majority to the People's Conference (PC) with 22 members while the other eight members were Independents. There was no necessity of having the three nominated members. Brig. T. Sailo took over as Chief Minister in June 1978. But his choice of Ministers brought about a split in the PC into PC(A) and PC (B). The intra-party conflict led to the resignation of eight PC members of the Assembly on October 13, 1978. The eight members along with the Speaker had also received the support of six other members who by that time had joined the Congress (four) and the Janata (two) and also one Independent. This left the ruling PC of Brig. Sailo with only 14 members which was clearly in a minority. Accordingly, Brig. Sailo resigned and recommended for the dissolution of the Assembly. The Assembly was dissolved on November 11, 1978.[177]

The mid-term elections were held in April 1979. This time again, the PC gained the majority but with a reduced number of 18, the Congress with five, two Janata and five Independents. Inspite of the defection of one of his Ministers, F. Malawma, to the Congress (I) Brig. Sailo could complete his five-year term.[178]

The General Elections of 1984 had reversed the fortunes of the PC, perhaps because of the incumbency factor, and the Congress (I), at the height of Indira Gandhi's popularity, secured an absolute majority with 20 seats. The PC could secure only eight seats while the

Independents won two seats. The Congress (I) ministry was sworn-in on May 3, 1984 with Lalthanhawla as the Chief Minister. But because of the Mizoram Peace Accord of June 20, 1986 between the Government of India and the MNF, Lalthanhawla could not complete his term.[179]

The Memorandum of Settlement (or Mizoram Peace Accord) of June 20, 1986 was followed by a political settlement on June 25, 1986 between Arjun Singh, Vice-President of AICC (I) and Lialdenga of the MNF. According to the political settlement, "the existing Congress (I) ministry shall be dissolved and the coalition ministry would be formed consisting of the MNF and the Congress headed by Laldenga. The MNF would have four seats and the Congress (I) five. The present Chief Minister Lalthanhawla would be the Deputy Chief Minister".[180] The MNF-Congress (I) coalition ministry under Laldenga was formed and continued till the General Elections of 1987.[181]

After the Peace Accord, the General Elections to the Mizoram Legislative Assembly, now with a 40-member House, were held on February 16, 1987. The results of the elections were:[182] MNF—24, Congress—13, and PC — three. After the elections, on February 20, 1987 four important events took place in Mizoram. At 7.00 A.M., Hiteswar Saikia was sworn-in as the Governor of Mizoram; at 7.30 A.M., Laldenga (MNF) was sworn-in as the Chief Minister of Mizoram thus ending the MNF-Congress (I) coalition ministry; at 10.30 A.M., the Prime Minister, Rajiv Gandhi, inaugurated Mizoram as the 23rd State of the Indian Union; and at 4.00 P.M., three Cabinet Ministers were sworn-in by the Governor.[183] Thus, ended the most busy day in the history of Mizoram. With the closing of that day, it may also be said that the era of coalition politics in the Mizoram Assembly had also come to an end so far as ministry-making was concerned.

The other aspects of coalition politics in the Mizoram Assembly, however, continued when on August 29, 1988 the 19-month old MNF ministry of Laldenga was reduced to a minority. Nine MNF legislators led by the Vice-President, Chawngzuala, formed a new party, the MNF

(Democratic).[184] Thus, there was an intra-party coalition in the MNF camp before the split. This intra-party coalition between the MNF (D) of Chawngzuala and the MPCC (I) of Lalthanhawla under the name and style of the United Legislative Party (ULP) staked its claim for an alternative coalition ministry in Mizoram.[185]

Meanwhile, the Speaker, J. Thangkuma had suspended the eight MNF(D) dissident members and asked them to show cause as to why they should not be disqualified as they fell short of the required number of 1/3 for a split, since the MNF by that time had a total strength of 25. However, the Deputy Speaker, K. Thanfianga who was in Boston (USA) for a medical treatment sent a message to the Speaker that he would join with the other eight members so as to make a group of nine dissidents. This would have met the required number of 1/3 for a split. But the message was not signed. Hence, the political crisis in the State had reached a deadlock where neither the MNF nor the opposition ULP coalition would be in a position to reach the magic number of 21. To end the political crisis, the Governor recommended to the Centre for a Proclamation of Emergency under Article 356 of the Indian Constitution. Accordingly, Mizoram was placed under the President's Rule on September 7, 1988 for a period of six months.[186]

The President's Rule was actually only for a period of five months. It was revoked on January 24, 1989 after the General Elections to the State Assembly on January 21, 1989. In the elections, the Congress (I) gained an absolute majority of 22 seats followed by MNF with 14, MNF (D)—two, and the PC with only one seat. One more seat remained undeclared at the time of the results. Lalthanhawla, the leader of the Congress (I) Legislature Party was sworn in as Chief Minister on January 24, 1989 after the revocation of the President's rule on the same day. The 1989 Congress (I) ministry continued to run the State Government till the end of its term.[187]

There were some political developments during the period before the next General Elections of 1993 to the State Assembly when a pre-poll alliance was arranged between the Congress (I) and the Mizoram Janata Dal (MJD). The MJD was the offshoot of the PC. During the 1993 elections, the Congress (I) and the MJD agreed to an electoral adjustment of 28 seats for the Congress (I) and the remaining 12 seats for the MJD. The elections were held on November 30, 1993 and the results were in favour of the Congress with 16 seats and eight seats for the MJD which formed a majority in the House. The MNF secured 14 while the two seats went to Independents.[188]

Lalthanhawla of the Congress (I) was again sworn-in as the Chief Minister in December 1993. But his ministry could not be purely a Congress (I) ministry since it could not become a majority all by itself. In addition to that there was also a pre-poll alliance with the MJD. At most, it may be called a Congress (I)-led coalition ministry. This ministry could also complete its full term when Mizoram went to the next General Elections on November 25, 1998.

The 1998 elections did not seem to be an easy one for the Congress (I) which had ruled the State for a decade now. The pre-poll opposition alliance between the MNF of Zoramthanga and the Mizoram People's Conference (MPC) which was earlier known as the MJD would definitely pose a serious challenge to the prospects of the Congress (I). The role played by the MPC (formerly MJD) led by Former Chief Minister, Brig. Sailo in the 1998 elections was a complete reversal of its 1993 pre-poll alliance with the Congress (I) and now in the 1998 elections with the MNF. Hence, it would be very interesting to watch out the outcome of this keenly contested elections in Mizoram.[189]

In the last seven General Elections ever since Mizoram became a Union Territory (1972) there were ups and downs in the fortunes of the regional as well as of the Congress Party. For twelve years (1972–1984) the regional parties under the MU and the PC had an edge over the Congress Party. The Congress could capture power only in May 1984 only to be replaced, due to political compulsion, by the MNF, another regional party, and followed by a short spell of President's Rule (September 1988 to January 1989). Ever since the 1989 General Elections, the Congress (I) had been commanding the confidence of the people of Mizoram due to the alleged failures of Brigadier Sailo's and Laldenga's regional parties. But now in 1998 the regional parties came round to criticise the failures of the Congress (I)'s 10-year rule.

The question now is where and what are really these failures anyway? After all, it is a fact that both Laldenga (MNF) and Lalthanhawla (Congress-I) had a coalition ministry during 1986–87; and the electoral alliance between Brig. Sailo (PC) and Lalthanhawla (Congress-I) in the 1993 General Elections which made Lalthanhawla's ministry a coalition ministry. And now, it seems that a third coalition, no longer between the regional and national parties, but between the regional parties themselves is emerging. We may now, for the present, await the outcome of the 1998 elections. In any case, in Mizoram it is not so much of political parties's role as the role of personalities which may decide whether their State politics is a coalition or not.

On December 3, 1998, a third coalition government of regional parties (United Legislature Party) between MNF (21) and MPC (12) has indeed been formed with Zoramthanga (MNF) as Chief Minister.

NAGALAND

The British relations with the Nagas started with the orders on November 13, 1866 of the Lieutenant Governor of Bengal constituting the Naga Hills District "consisting of that part of the district of Nowgong which lies on the right bank of the river Dhansiri, the Naga Hills and the country on both banks of the river Doyang".[190] Lt. J. Gregory, officer in-charge of North Cachar sub-division was appointed as the Deputy Commissioner of the new district.[191] However, in 1872 under the Rules for Administration of Justice, the Naga Hills was called an "agency" and the Deputy Commissioner was renamed the "Political Agent".[192] But, after the occupation of Kohima and

Wokha in 1878 the "political control" gave way to "administrative control" by the creation of the new Naga Hills District for Naga Hills with the headquarters at Kohima on April 24, 1882 and the title of the Political Agent was restored to that of the Deputy Commissioner.[193]

The administration of the district of Naga Hills was as per provisions of the Bengal Eastern Frontier Regulation, 1873 where beyond the Inner Line "the tribes were left to manage their own affairs with only such interference on the part of the frontier officers in their political capacity as may be considered advisable with a view to establishing a personal influence for good among the Chiefs and the tribes."[194] The Scheduled Districts Act, 1874 was also applicable to Naga Hills district where General Acts and Regulations would be restricted in the "backward tracts".[195] The Naga Hills was also excluded from the reforms under the Government of India Act, 1915. The Naga Club which was formed in 1918 was also demanding for being excluded from the Reforms under the Government of India Act 1935.[196] Accordingly, the Naga Hills was declared an Excluded Area and had no representation in the Assam Legislative Council nor in the Assam Legislative Assembly.

This position continued until the coming of India's independence when the Naga leader, Angami Zapu Phizo, under the banner of the Naga National Council (NNC) declared Naga's independence on August 14, 1947. The NNC was formed in 1946 having its origin in the Naga District Tribal Council of 1945 as a body for the Nagas to decide their future after the Transfer of British Power. The declaration of Naga independence was followed by a Naga plebiscite in May 1951 which gave an overwhelming majority support for Naga independence. In between, the Constituent Assembly of India accepted the recommendation of the Bordoloi Committee for the inclusion of Naga Hills district under the Sixth Schedule to the Constitution of India with an autonomous district council of their own.

Unlike the other hill areas of Assam, the leaders of Naga Hills had outrightly rejected the Sixth Schedule.

Simultaneously, there was also a provision in the Constitution of India for their representation in the Assam Legislative Assembly with three members to be elected by an adult franchise. The Nagas did not accept this provision either and had boycotted all the General Elections to the Assam Legislative Assembly and to the Indian Parliament in 1952 and 1957. In 1957, the Government of India made an attempt to constitute the Naga Hills Tuensang Area (NHTA) under a Commissioner to be assisted by Deputy Commissioners. This arrangement also did not satisfy the aspiration of the Nagas for independence. It was in 1960 that a decision was made to have an interim arrangement for the future political status of NHTA. By the Nagaland (Transitional Provisions) Regulation, 1962 an Interim body was constituted with 45 members to be elected according to the "customs and usages" of the Naga tribes.[197]

The Interim Body, headed by a President, would have an Executive Council of five members to be headed by a Chairman. Imkongliba Ao was the President of the Interim Body, and P. Shilu Ao the Chairman of the Executive Council; while Jasokie represented the Angamis and Hokishe Ṣema the Semas. The Executive Council was advisory in nature and therefore its status was much less than the Council of Ministers.[198]

The Interim Body was meant to be for a period of three years. But the series of incidents and deteriorating political situations resulting in the assassination of Imkongliba-Ao, the President of the Interim body, made the Government of India to speed up the process of the creation of the Nagaland State. By the 13th Amendment to the Indian Constitution the State of Nagaland was created; and on December 1, 1963 the State of Nagaland was inaugurated by the President of India, Dr. Radhakrishnan. The Chairman of the earlier Executive Council of the Interim Body became the first Chief Minister.[199] In passing, it may be said that the composition of the Executive Council of the Interim Body and subsequently the provisional Council of Ministers had reflected the politics of coalition not on party lines but on tribal considerations in view of the fact that Nagaland was and is an heterogeneous political society.

Immediately after the creation of the Nagaland State, the First General Elections were held during January 10-16, 1964.[200] There were 46 elected seats including six members to be indirectly elected by the Regional Council of Tuensang Area. Nagaland had the distinction of being the only State in North-East India which was broadly having a two-party system. In the 1964 General Elections to the First Assembly it was a fight between the two regional parties, the Naga Nationalist Organisation (NNO) which grew out of the Naga People's Convention (NPC) which had spearheaded both the NHTA and the full-fledged State of Nagaland on one side, and the Democratic Party of Nagaland (DPN) on the other. True, the Independents were also there in the fray. Another unique feature of Nagaland politics that had followed from a two-party system was that there was little room for coalition politics in the State at least at the party level in the initial stages.

In the 1964 elections the NNO captured an absolute majority with 33 seats and the DPN with 11 seats while the Independents won two seats. These figures also included those six members who were indirectly elected by the Regional Council of Tuensang Area. The NNO formed the ministry with P. Shilu Ao as Chief Minister.[201] But for some political and personal reasons the P. Shilu Ao NNO ministry was voted out by his own NNO colleagues and after a vote of no-confidence from the Treasury Bench itself, a practice which was unheard of in any parliamentary system of Government anywhere else in the world, was carried out. T.N. Angami (NNO) formed his ministry in 1966 which continued till the 1969 General Elections.[202] In the 1969 Second General Elections the same performance was repeated by the NNO. The results were NNO—20, United Front of Nagaland (UNF)—10, and eight Independents. The NNO was joined by the 12 MLAs (raised from six) of Tuensang Area and one Independent making a total of 33 again. Naturally, the NNO formed the ministry which may be called a coalition ministry with Hokishe Sema as Chief Minister. Yet another coalition at the inter-party level took place in 1972 when the UFN was joined by 14 NNO legislators and this coalition was known as the United Democratic Front (UDF), under the leadership of Vizol.[203]

The strength of the State Assembly which was fixed at 46 was raised to 52 in 1969 and again raised to 60 in 1974. In the Third General Elections, the UDF secured 25, NNO—23, and 12 Independents. Seven Independents joined the UDF and four with the NNO. The UDF with 32 members which was clearly a coalition majority formed the ministry with Vizol as Chief Minister. But in March 1975 the Vizol ministry was defeated due to defection. The coalition ministry led by J.B. Jasokie survived only for 10 days due to further defection. President's Rule had, therefore, to be imposed which continued for 32 months. During the President's Rule, the NNO merged itself with the Congress Party and for the first time in the history of Nagaland the national party had entered into Nagaland Politics.[204]

The Fourth General Elections took place in November 1977. The UDF secured 35 seats, Congress—15, one Nationalist Council of Nagaland (NCN) and nine Independents. Most of the Independents joined the UDF. Vizol formed his second ministry but was toppled in April, 1980.[205]

After the fall of the Vizol's ministry, some MLAs formed the Naga National Party (NNP) under Jasokie's leadership. The remaining 28 UDF legislators joined in a coalition with the NNP and formed the Naga National Democratic Party (NNDP). So in June 1980 the NNDP ministry was installed with J.B. Jasokie as Chief Minister, The NNDP coalition ministry remained in power till the Fifth General Elections in 1982.[206] It may be noted that Huska Sumri (UDF) refused to join the NNDP and formed his Naga People's Party (NPP).[207]

During the Fifth General Elections, 1982 the results were Congress(I) with 24 seats, NNDP 24 and 12 Independents. The Congress (I) formed the coalition ministry with the help of Independents.[208] It was in the Sixth

General Elections, 1987 that the results went in favour of the Congress(I) with 31 seats, NNDP—15, and one NPP and seven Independents.[209] Naturally the Congress (I) formed the ministry under Hokishe Sema as Chief Minister and the NNDP remained in the opposition.[210] But in the first week of July 1988, 13 Congress (I) legislators defected from or caused a split in the party, thereby reducing the Congress (I) into a minority. This political situation resulted in the downfall of the Sema's Congress ministry. These 13 Congress (I) MLAs joined hands with the NNDP under the new party called the Nagaland People's Council (NPC, to be differentiated with the earlier NPC of the Naga People's Convention) with a view to form a coalition ministry. But this could not be materialised as the President's Rule was imposed in the State in August 1988.[211]

The next General Elections to the State Assembly was held on January 21, 1989. The results were in favour of the Congress (I) with 36 seats and the NPC with 24 seats.[212] The new Congress(I) ministry with S.C. Jamir as Chief Minister was sworn-in in January 1990.[213] But because of defections and/or split, the NPC was in a position to wrest power from the Congress (I) after one year. Thus, in May 1990, the NPC ministry was formed with K.L. Chishi as Chief Minister but could last barely a month in office.[214] It was during that time that there was an understanding among the various groups in the Assembly to form the Joint Legislator Party which captured power in June 2, 1990 with Vamuzo as Chief Minister.[215] The Vamuzo coalition Government could continue in office till the General Elections to the State Assembly in 1993.

The next General Elections for the Nagaland Legislative Assembly were held on February 15, 1993. In the elections, the Congress (I) secured 35 seats, and the NPC—18. The remaining seven seats went to the Independents. The Congress (I) once again formed the ministry with S.C. Jamir as Chief Minister in February 1993.[216] The Jamir ministry could complete its full term in February 1998.

The recent General Elections to the State Assembly were held in February 1998. The 1998 elections in Nagaland were very unique in character. Perhaps the electoral process of 1998 that had taken place in Nagaland had no parallel in North East India nor earlier been in Nagaland itself. It was for the first time that out of 60 seats, 34 Congress (I) candidates were elected unopposed on February 4, 1998. The other political parties like the Naga Democratic Movement under Vamuzo, the BJP and the NPC did not set up any candidate.

The main reason for such a poll boycott was that in view of the fact that the peace-talk between the Government of India and the National Socialist Council of Nagaland (NSCN) of Issac-Muivah (I-M) group was continuing, there was, therefore, a request from the political parties, other than the Congress (I) to postpone the elections. Another reason, and perhaps, the real reason was because of the poll-boycott call by the Naga Non-Governmental Organisations including the Naga Hoho Summit of the NSCN (I-M) and the Naga Mothers' Association. In response to such a call for a poll-boycott, the candidates from political parties, other than the Congress (I) and the Independents, did not file their nomination for the elections.[217]

On February 7, 1998 the Congress (I) again won nine more seats, the nine Independent candidates having withdrawn from the contest. Thus, the tally for the Congress (I) came to 43 as on the last date for the withdrawing of candidature. The pollings for the 17 remaining seats were held on February 23, 1998 between the Congress (I) and the Independent candidates.[218] The Congress (I) having an absolute majority formed the Government with S.C. Jamir as Chief Minister in February, 1998. One important point to be noted in this connection was that, immediately before the actual election process started, the NSCN (I-M) had withdrawn its call for a poll-boycott. But by that time only the Congress (I), barring a few Independent candidates, were in the field. But this is another aspect of coalition politics in Nagaland which is outside the purview of this Lecture.

Thus, in the 35-year history of electoral politics in Nagaland there were 12 Governments including three clear cut cases of coalition ministries of the UDF coalition in 1974 under Vizol, the NNDP coalition in 1977 under J.B. Jasokie, and the JLP coalition in 1990 under Vamuzo. In between there was also the President's Rule during 1988–89. Of course, the element of coalition politics in Nagaland could be traced right from the time of the Interim Body of 1960 based on the consideration of communities rather than on a coalition of political parties.

Another landmark in Nagaland coalition politics was in the First General Elections of 1964 when there was an intra-party coalition in the ruling NNO of P. Shilu Ao and of T.N. Angami. Here again if we go deeper into this intra-party coalition in the NNO, it was based mainly on community consideration rather than on coalition politics *per se*. Even the UDF coalition ministry of 1974 was in fact the fusion of the two intra-party coalition of the UFN and the breakaway Legislators. Another intraparty coalition was the fusion of the breakaway NNP and the breakaway UDF to form the NNDP.

Inspite of these developments in the field of coalition politics in Nagaland we may still say that by and large the trend in Nagaland is towards developing a two-party system right from the beginning. In the beginning it was between two regional parties, the NNO and the DPN. Hence, these political parties being regional in character cannot be said that they had strong opposite ideologies. Even when the two party system, later on, was between the regional party and the national party, the latter was still not free from regional considerations. This happens because Nagaland is more heterogeneous in character with the three main communities—The Angamis, Aos, and Semas playing the dominant role. In fact, it is a land with a larger number of Naga communities not only in Nagaland, but also in Arunachal Pradesh, Assam, Manipur and across the international border of Myanmar. It cannot be compared with Arunachal Pradesh which is equally heterogeneous in character, because for quite sometime now only one community, the Adis, dominated the political scene, though the Nishis are also coming up.

When all is said and done, Nagaland provides an interesting field of study for coalition politics even within the framework of the two party system. We are still watching, with great interest, the further developments on whether the two-party system will give way to a one-party dominance under the Congress(I) after the General Elections of February 1998; and pondering on whether any intra-party coalition will develop within the Congress (I) before the next General Elections in 2003. It all depends on whether the process of electoral politics is free and fair enough.

TRIPURA

The British interest in Tripura began in early 1761 after Maharaja Krishna Manyika had a dispute with them in 1760. On January 20, 1761 Governor Vansittart of Islamabad Factory had issued an instruction for action against the ruler of Tripura. Verlest, the Chief of Islamabad British Factory despatched Lieutenant Mathews with 200 sepoys and two guns to Tripura on February 25, 1761. The British Force was so overwhelming for Maharaja Krishna Manyika that he preferred to submit and the British flag was raised over Tripura.[219] Within one month, on March 15, Ralp Leeke was appointed the first Resident of Tripura, and the subjugation of Tripura was completed.[220]

As a matter of fact it was because of the dispute between Bengal and Tripura over the Zamindary of Chakla Roshnabad that had brought the British into Tripura. But the British could not influence Tripura very much during the Residency.[221] It was only when Tripura was placed under a Political Agent in 1871 that the British had wielded much influence beginning with the reign of Maharaja Birchandra Manyika.[222] With the advice of the Political Agent Maharaja Birchandra introduced administrative reforms between 1876 and 1896 patterned on the British model. He had even sought the help of officers from British India to help him with his administrative reforms. He also established a Council of Ministers in place of the Dewan.[223] It was the beginning of the joint Anglo-Tripura administration of the State.

From 1897 to 1909, Maharaja Radhakishore introduced the Executive and Legislative Councils as well as the Advisory Council.[224] His successor, Maharaja Bindra -Kishore (1909-23) made further improvements in the administration by constituting the State Council with official and non official representations.[225]

Gradually, Tripura had fallen completely under the tutelage of the British. The last ruling Maharaja Bir Bikram Kishore Manyika (1927–47) who was regarded as the most enlightened ruler of Tripura had further made an attempt to decentralise the administration by constituting three bodies for a better administration—the Advisory Council (*Mantranne Sabha*), the Legislative Council *(Byabasthapak Sabha)*, and the Executive Council *(Mantri Parisath)*. The Advisory Council under the title of the State Council could even run the administration during the absence of the Maharaja. The Mandal Act was also passed for the self-administration of the tribal areas. At the apex of all these structural reforms was the Central Assembly. In 1939, Maharaja Bir Bikram had also declared a semi-popular constitution for the State but could not be implemented due to the outbreak of the Second World War.[226]

After the death of Maharaja Bir Bikram, his son and successor Kirit Bikram became the Maharaja of Tripura. But being a minor, a council of Regency was constituted under the Presidentship of his mother, Maharani Kanchan Prava Devi. But because of great internal crisis in the State due to the attempts of the Muslims to annex Tripura to Pakistan, the Government of India advised the dissolution of the Counil of Regency and Maharani Kanchan Prava Devi became the sole Regent on January 12, 1948.[227]

Since then, the political developments in the State moved faster in the direction of Tripura's merger with the Indian Union. The Tripura Merger Agreement was signed in New Delhi by the Maharani on September 9, 1949 in her capacity as the Regent of Tripura. In accordance with the Agreement, Tripura became a part C State of India, and its administration was placed under the Chief Commissioner on October 15, 1949.[228] But the Zamindary of Chakla Roshnabad with which began the British contact in 1761 did not remain in Tripura as it was included in East Pakistan.[229]

The first modern elections in Tripura were held on December 17, 1945 to the Agartala Municipality during the reign of Maharaja Bir Bikram. During the 1945 elections there was no participation by the political parties, as they were still in their nascent and dormant stage. It was only after the demise of Maharaja Bir Bikram on May 17, 1947 and after India's independence that political parties had "openly" and "desperately" started their active participation in the electoral politics of the State.[230]

After its merger with India on October 15,1949, Tripura was made a Part C State of the Indian Union under the Part C State (Laws) Act, 1950 to be centrally administered by a Chief Commissioner. Simultaneously, under the 1950 Act, provisions were also made for a Legislature and a nominated Council of Advisors for Tripura.

The advises of the Council of Advisors (Council of Ministers) were, however, not binding on the Chief Commissioner.[231] In the 1952 General Elections for an electoral College for the Lok Sabha and the Legislative Assembly elections, the CPI secured 12 seats, Congress—nine, six Independents, and three Tripura Ganatantric Sangh (TGS) making a total of 30 members.[232] Being Centrally administered, the results went against the CPI as the Union Government under the Congress ministry had naturally to favour the State Congress and tried to suppress the Communists.[233] Later on, the Advisory Council was formed by the Union Government by an Order of the President on April 15, 1953 with three Advisors. Two of the Advisors were the prominent Congress leaders of Tripura and the third one was a retired Tripuri Government servant.[234]

In 1956, the States Reorganisation Commission recommended for the creation of Union Territories in place of those centrally administered territories like Tripura. In the same year the Part C State (Laws) Act, 1950 was modified as the Union Territories (Laws) Act, 1956.[235] The Union Territories (Laws) Act 1956 was followed by the Seventh Amendment of the Constitution of India, by altering Article 239. Under this constitutional Amendment, the Territorial Councils Act, 1956 was passed. The Act of 1956 made a provision for a Territorial Council and also an Advisory Committee for Tripura.[236] The strength of the Council was 30 elected members by adult franchise and two members to be nominated by the President of India. The Territorial Council had a Chairman to be elected by the Council and the Chief Executive Officer to be appointed by the Chief Commissioner, redesignated as Administrator.[237]

Thus, the Congress Party was dominating the political scene of Tripura ever since its accession to the Indian Union. In the four subsequent General Elections in 1957, 1962, 1967, and 1972 the Congress captured the majority and formed the Congress ministries for over a decade.[238] The two Congress veterans Sachindra Lal Singh and Sijhamoy Sen Gupta were the Chief Ministers during that period.[239] To indicate the political influence of the Congress Party in Tripura, the results of the four elections were as follows:[240]

	1957 Elections	1962 Elections	1967 Elections (18th February)	1972 Elections (11th March)
Congress	15	17	27	41
CPI	12	13	1	1
TGS	1	30		
CPI(M)			2	17
Independents	2		30	1
Total	30			60

Thus, with the help of the non-communist parties and Independents the Congress could take over power in 1957. Besides, there were two nominated members to support the Congress. In the next three elections, the Congress secured an absolute majority in the 1962, 1967 and 1972 elections. In addition, the number of nominated members had been increased from two to three in 1963. The problem, however, was with the two veteran Congress leaders, Singh and Sen Gupta, who were fighting between themselves. Their differences led to the imposition of the President's Rule in the State in December 1971 for four months till the General Elections on March 11, 1972. Thus, inspite of the Congress ministries in Tripura, till 1977 it may be said that there were intra-party coalitions because of the two Congress leaders. It was the intra-party coalitions in the Congress fold during that period which had brought its own downfall when the 1977 elections were held.

In passing it may be noted that the Territorial Council of Tripura was renamed the Legislative Assembly under the Union Territories (Amendment) Act, 1963. In addition to the Legislative Assembly, a provision was also made for a Council of Ministers.[241] Again, on December 30, 1971 the North-Eastern Areas (Reorganisation) Act was passed and upgraded Tripura from its Union Territory status to that of a full-fledged State. Under the 1971 Act, the Administrator was renamed the Lieutenant Governor;[242] and the strength of the Legislative Assembly was raised from 30 (with two nominated members upto 1962 and three since 1963) to 60 members to be elected through an adult franchise.

Before the 1977 General Elections and the downfall of the Congress ministry, there were attempts by Singh and Sen Gupta to form their own coalition ministry. Sen Gupta wanted to form a Coalition Government with the defectors from the Congress and the CPI(M) on the night of March 29, 1977. But Singh immediately agreed to all the conditions put forward by the CPI(M) which had enabled him to form the first coalition Janata Party in Tripura on April 1, 1977, with Prafulla Das of the CFD as the Chief Minister along with the 13-member CFD dissident group and the CPI(M). The coalition ministry lasted upto

July 25, 1977 and the second Janata-CPI(M) coalition ministry was led by Radhika Ranjan Gupta (Janata) from July 26, 1977 to December 31, 1977.[243] It was these two coalition ministries in which the CPI(M) had associated or coalesced itself that had brought a rich dividend in its electoral prospects for the General Elections on December 31, 1977.

The 1977 elections to the Tripura Assembly were held amidst "political anarchy, turmoil, chaos and confusion".[244] The Congress was already a divided house. Its votes were actually shared by the Congress, CFD, Janata, Tripura Upajati Juba Samity (TUJS) and the Independents. Only the Leftists could form a grand coalition in order to avoid a division of their votes. Besides, the Leftists were already in power in the two consecutive coalition ministries led by Das (CFD) and Gupta (Janata) from April 1 to December 31, 1977.[245] Thus, as expected, the results were an outstanding victory for the Leftists coalition under the CPI(M) with 53 seats out of 60. The remaining seven seats were shared by TUJS— four, RSP— two, and one Independent.[246] In January 1978, Nripen Chakraborty became the Chief Minister of the CPI (M)-led Left front coalition and completed his term till the next General Elections in 1983.

The 1983 General Elections were marked by the deterioration of law and order due to the Tripura National Volunteers' (TNV) extremism.[247] Because of acts of violence occurring during the Left Front regime, the masses tended to turn to the Congress. But the Congress itself was again a divided house. That was why the Left Front could emerge victorious in the elections. The CPI(M) secured 37 seats followed by the Congress(I)—12, TUJS-six, and RSP—two. The other results of the three remaining seats were declared later on. The Left Front coalition ministry again assumed power for a full form with Nripen Chakraborty (CPI-M) as the Chief Minister.

The next General Elections were held on February 2, 1988. But this time the Left Front had failed to continue in power, the CPI(M) could secure only 26 seats and the RSP—two. The Congress(I) though having polled less than the CPI(M) with 25 seats yet it could manage to form the ministry with the support of the seven TUJS in accordance with the pre-poll alliance arrangement between the two parties. The Congress (I)-TUJS coalition could, therefore, bring about the working majority under the leadership of S. Ranjan Majumdar (Congress-I) as the Chief Minister.[248] Though the claim was made to be the Congress(I) ministry, yet because of the support of the TUJS, it may still be categorised as a coalition ministry, at least a legislative coalition, if not an executive legislation.

The Congress(I) internal dissension and the further deteriorating law and order situation made it an easy target for criticism by the Left Front opposition. On February 15, 1993 the next General Elections took place. This time, the strength of the Congress(I) was therefore reduced to 10 seats only. The results were as follows:[249]

Congress(I)	: 10	Forward Bloc	: 1	
CPI(M)	: 44	TUJS	: 1	
RSP	: 2			
Janata Dal(B) (Janata Party till 1988)	: 1	Total	: 59	(one seat was declared later on)

Thus, the Left Front came again to power with an absolute majority. Dasarath Deb(CPI-M) took over power as Chief Minister of the Left Front coalition government.

The Left Front coalition for the fourth time took over power on March 11, 1998 with Manik Sarkar (CPI-M) as the Chief Minister after the General Elections which were held on February 11, 1998. The Left Front secured 41 seats followed by 19 opposition Front of the Congress, TUJS, TNV, and one Independent.[250] At the time of writing, the Left Front appears to be quite comfortable in its saddle as the process of coalition politics among the Left Front partners is more stable than the process of coalition politics among the Congress(I) and its partners. From its earlier experiences and its present stability, the Left Front coalition government may even last till the next General Elections in 2003.

Over the years, it has been observed that in Tripura, as in Arunachal Pradesh and Nagaland, the trend is towards developing a two-party system—the Congress and Communists. But unlike the other two States, where one-party dominance is, of late, emerging, in Tripura it is a straight contest between the two national parties. Of course, the regional parties and Independents, at times, had played the role of a balancer by enabling one political party or the other to come to power.

The role of the regional party, the TUJS may be mentioned in this connection. There was a time during the seventies when it had extended its support to the Left Front; while at other times it was aligning or coalescing itself during the 1988 elections with the Congress as well as in the recent 1998 elections. But, it is only when the two main national political parties are equally poised that the TUJS can play its role of a balancer, leading to the formation of coalition governments in the State.

However, coalition politics in Tripura, as in Arunachal Pradesh, is not that much conspicuous as in the other remaining five States of North-East India. This is due to the fact that till 1972 the Congress was dominating the political scene of Tripura, and since 1977 the CPI(M) had become a strong contender for political power in the State. Only for a brief period in 1977, the Janata Party coalition governments of Prafulla Das(CFD) and Radhika Ranjan Gupta (CPI-M) could break the monopoly of power by only one of the two main national parties.

The CPI(M) dominance since 1977 was broken in 1988 when it could not form the government inspite of the fact that it was the single largest party with 26 seats in the House. The Congress(I) with 25 seats had managed to form another coalition ministry with the help and support of the TUJS.

Of late, Tripura has been continually facing acute ethnic problems in the hill areas. This problem has put both the Congress and the Communists in a very difficult situation. To that extent coalition politics in the State has been diluted, as the TUJS, the TNV or any other regional parties may not be in a position to cause any difference in the power struggle between the two main national parties. The recent pattern of electoral politics in the State is that either one or the other of the national parties could capture power depending on which ruling party would be at the Centre.

It is also interesting to note that when neither of the national parties would be in power at the Centre, either by sheer co-incidence or by design, the ruling party in Tripura would follow the West Bengal pattern of coalition politics among the Leftists. Thus, in the present set up of the Union Government, the Left Front coalition in Tripura may as well continue in completing its full term. Until then, not only the Left Front coalition would continue to exist but the Congress(I) also may have to forge ahead with an arrangement for an inter-party coalition to wrest power from the Left Front coalition government.

A RECAPITULATION

We have now come to the end of our attempt to trace out the development of coalition politics in North-East India ever since India's independence. A brief description of the cause of political events leading to the process of coalition politics in each political unit of the region has been given. At the end of such descriptive accounts certain observations have also been made. While making our observations, a certain amount of analysis of the underlying causes and principles of such coalition politics has also been explained. As the course of coalition politics in North-East India is still a continuing phenomenon, no tentative conclusion even can be given at this stage. However, a recapitulation of what has been discussed in Part III of this lecture may be briefly stated.

The seed of coalition politics which had been sown in Assam politics during the British period, as well as in the Native States of Manipur and Tripura when the British element of politics and administration were partly introduced, has not only germinated, bloomed, flowered and borne some fruits during the period but also has produced more seeds in the post-independence period in all the seven sister States of North-East India. Some of them like Meghalaya, have experienced coalition politics right from their inception, while others are adopting it at a later stage. But all of them, with no exception, have in the course of time to resort to such coalition formation. Arunachal Pradesh tried its best to avoid it, but technically there is a coalition politics there too.

In Assam, the similar process of coalition politics has been revived again as in the British period essentially because of the differences between the two valleys and the Hindu-Muslim divide as well as the problems of other ethnic communities both in the hills and the plains. The Congress Party was in a position to contain the process of intra-party coalition politics for about three decades. But the intra-party politics in the Congress camp continues. Intra-party politics continues in the other parties of the State as well.

In the hilly ares of Nagaland, Meghalaya and Mizoram where separate States from Assam have been created during the sixties, seventies, and eighties respectively, coalition politics has been in existence either due to communities consideration or because of the imperative of political consideration. But the role of political ideology in the coalition politics in the hilly States is less pronounced compared to the role of political ideology as in the States of Assam and Tripura. Mizoram is in a slightly better position since it is more or less a socially homogenous State. But all the same, coalition politics in these three States has centred around personality and community considerations rather than on political ideology.

The erstwhile native States of Manipur and Tripura, on the other hand, have to start the process of coalition politics not through their experience during the British period, but after their accession to India and because of political compulsion. As in the other States of the region, the process of coalition politics in these two States has also more or less followed the pattern of what is happening at the Centre, particularly after the era of coalition politics has prevailed at the national level.

Arunachal Pradesh is a category by itself. It comes very late in the political spectrum of North East India. But within a decade after India's independence, it has picked up the process of electoral politics very fast, perhaps even faster than the other States and communities in the region. Though the State is socially heterogeneous in character, yet it has been able to maintain its political stability due essentially to the dominant position of one community and of one party. However, indications are there, that this State too may join the fate of other hilly States so far as the course of coalition politics is concerned.

All the States, whenever the need for a coalition politics arises, have followed one or the other type, pattern, and level ranging from a pre-poll alliance to a post-poll alliance; from intra-party to inter-party coalitions; from legislative, executive, governmental to responsive, grand and federal coalitions. Thus, while going through the process of coalition politics in each State discussed above, one may find out the examples of all kinds of known coalition politics so far practiced in the parliamentary system of Government. Perhaps, it may be a truism to say that other States in the country, nay in the other parts of the world, may have to share something from North-East India's experience like a lottery coalition government and 50 : 50 basis of power sharing in the coalition governments.

Regarding the question of stability of coalition ministries in the region, by and large, the political conditions are not suitable for such a stability. Apart from the consideration of insurgency activities, ethnic movements, and pressures of castes and communities, personalities also play an important role in the stability or otherwise of any coalition ministry. Besides, coalition politics in North-East India has not strictly followed either the game theory or the policy-based theory. Even in an ideologically-based politics of Tripura, we notice the abandonment of the policy-based theory in favour of a game theory in its Janata Party coalitions. After 50 years of the course of coalition politics in North East India, we may say that it has not become stabilized so far. It requires the institutionalisation of coalition politics in order that its stability may be ensured in future.

All the discussions in the present series of these Lectures are confined mainly to the coalition politics at the State Legislative Assembly level. It would be only right and proper to have a further study on coalition politics at the level of parliamentary electoral politics of the region as well as at the levels of the municipalities, local boards, autonomous district councils, autonomous regional councils, and village councils. This has to be done by future research scholars in order to have a complete picture of coalition politics in North-East India.

NOTES AND REFERENCES

THEORETICAL CONSIDERATION

1. See *Encyclopaedia Americana,* (New York, 1972), Vol. 21, p. 487; *Encyclopaedia Britannica,* (London, 1973), Vol. 17, pp. 538–541; and Hammond, N.G.L., *A History of Greece to 322 B.C.,* (Clarendon Press, Oxford, London, 1973), Reprinted, pp. 482–91; and Elrenberg, Victor, *The Greek State,* (Methnen and Co., London, 1974), Reprinted, pp. 111–121.
2. *Encyclopaedia Americana,* 1972, Vol. 2, p. 81. See also Mommsen, Theodor, *The History of Rome,* (MacMillan, London, 1908), Vol. IV, pp. 378; 504–505 who had referred to two other triumvirates or (i) coalition in 683 between Caesar (democracy) and two Generals Gnaeus Pompeius and Marcus Crassus (military); and (ii) coalition in 693 between Caesar and his ally Crassus (democracy) and Pompeius (capitalist). On a closer examination these two triumvirates appear to refer to the same triumvirate though different in dates. Similarly, the Julius Caesar of *Encyclopaedia Americana* (44 B.C.) seems to be different from Gaius Julius Caesar (born 652 or 654) of Mommsen (p. 278).
3. Gupta, S.P., and Ramachandran, K.S., (eds.), *Myth and Reality,* (Agam Prakashan, Delhi, 1976), p. ix.
4. Sarkar, Khhimuddin, *Aspects of Historical Geography of Pragjyotisa Kamrupa: Ancient Assam,* (Naya Prakash, Calcutta, 1992), p. 13.

5. F.N. 2.
6. Kashyap, Subhash C., *The Politics of Power: Defection and State Politics in India,* (National Publishing House, New Delhi, 1975) p. 19; See also Kashyap, Subhash C., *The Politics of Defection: A Study of State Politics in India,* (National Publishing House, Delhi, 1969), p. 422.
7. *Ibid.,* (1975), and (1969), p. 423.
8. *Ibid.,* (1975), and (1969).
9. *Ibid.,* (1975), and (1969).
10. *Ibid.,* (1975), and (1969).
11. *Ibid.,* (1975), and (1969).
12. *Ibid.,* (1975), p. 100.
13. *Oxford English Dictionary,* (Clarendon Press, Oxford, London, 1961), Reprinted, Vol. II, p. 552.
14. *Random House of English Language,* (Tulsi Shah Enterprises, Bombay, 1970), p. 282.
15. Riker, William H., "The Study of Coalitions", in *Encyclopaedia of Social Sciences,* (MacMillan, New York, 1972), Reprint, Vol. 2, p. 524.
16. *Ibid.*
17. *Ibid.*
18. *Ibid.*
19. Gamson, William A., "Coalition Formation", in *Encyclopaedia of Social Sciences,* (1972), p. 530.
20. *Ibid.,* p. 531.
21. Lijphart, Arend, *Democracy in Plural Societies: A Comparative Exploration,* (Popular Prakashan, Bombay, 1989), Indian Reprint.
22. Eckstein, Harry, *Division and Cohesion in a Democracy,* (Princeton University Press, Princeton, 1966), p. 34.
23. Lewis, W. Arthur, *Politics in West Africa,* (Allen and Unwin, London, 1965, especially chapter 3. cited in Lijphart, Arend, *op. cit.,* p. 144.
24. *Ibid.,*
25. *Ibid.,* p. 145.
26. See Pakem, B., "Electoral Politics in North-East India and Development in Political Theory", in *Proceedings of the North-East India Political Science Association,* Sixth Annual Conference Dibrugarh University, (Dibrugarh), December 1996, p. 8.
27. Lijphart, Arend, *op. cit.,* p. 164.
28. *Ibid.,* p. 236.
29. *Ibid.,* p. 232.
30. Kothari, Rajni, *Politics in India,* (Orient Longmans, Ltd. New Delhi, 1970), p. 192.

31. *Ibid.*, p. 183.
32. *Ibid.*, p. 190.
33. *Ibid.*, p. 429.
34. *Ibid.*
35. *Ibid.*, p. 428.
36. *Ibid.*
37. *Ibid.*, p. 437.
38. *Ibid.*
39. Khare, Harish, "Coalition Politics", *Seminar* (New Delhi, No. 377, January, 1991), p. 37.
40. Sridharan, E., "Coalition Politics", *Seminar,* (New Delhi, No. 437), January, 1996), p. 54.
41. Desai, A.R., *State and Society in India: Essays in Dissent,* (Popular Prakashan, Bombay, 1975), p. 178.
42. Singh, Raghuveer, "Coalition Politics: Some Considerations", in Karunnakaram, K.P., (ed.), *Coalition Governments in India: Problems and Prospects,* (Indian Institute of Advanced Study, Shimla, 1975), p. 47.
43. Minocha, O.P., "Coalition Government: Experience and Prospects", A Theme Paper during the 40th Members' Annual Conference of the Indian Institute of Public Administration, (New Delhi, 1996, unpublished), p. 2.
44. Cited by Roy, Ash Narain, in "Stress on Consensus", *Hindustan Times,* (New Delhi, April 2, 1998) Editorial Page.
45. Kothari, Rajni, *op. cit.*, p. 153.
46. *Ibid.*, p. 303.
47. Riker, William, H., *op. cit.*, p. 72; See also Gupta, R.L., *The Politics of Commitment,* (Trimurti Publications, New Delhi), 1972, pp. 52–53.
48. Riker, William, H., *op. cit.*, p. 72.
49. *Ibid.*
50. *Ibid.*, p. 75; See also Weiner, Myron, *Party Politics in India: The Development of a Multi-Party System,* (Princeton University Press, Princeton, 1957), p. 56.
51. Riker, William H., *op. cit.*, p. 75.
52. *Ibid.*, p. 76.
53. *Ibid.*
54. Daṇdavate, Madhu, "Coalition Politics in India", in *Politics India,* (New Delhi, February, 1997), Vol. 1, No. 8, p. 9.
55. *Shillong Times,* April 1, 1998.
56. Rao, V. Venkata and Hazarika, Niru, *A Century of Government and Politics in North East India, 1874–1980,* Vol. I (Assam), (S. Chand and Company, New Delhi, 1983), p. 148.
57. *Seminar,* (New Delhi, No. 298, July, 1984), p. 12.

58. *Ibid.*, p. 13.
59. Cited by Singh, L.P., "Learning from Experience", in a *Coalition Future, Seminar,* (New Delhi, No. 298, July, 1984), p. 15.
60. *Hindustan Times,* (New Delhi), April 2, 1998, Editorial page.
61. Singh, L.P., *op. cit.,* p. 18.
62. *Ibid.*, p. 16.
63. Kothari, Rajni, *op. cit.*, p. 153.
64. Sen, Mohit, "Coalition Politics", *Politics India,* (New Delhi, March 1997), Vol. I, No. 9, p. 24.
65. *Ibid.*
66. Namboodripad, E.M.S., "Means to an End", *Seminar,* (New Delhi, No. 298, July 1984), p. 21.
67. Kothari, Rajni, *op. cit.,* p. 171.
68. *Ibid.*, p. 173.
69. *Ibid.*, p. 175.
70. *Ibid.*, p. 182.
71. *Ibid.*, p. 305.
72. *Ibid.*, p. 431.
73. *Shillong Times,* April 1, 1998.
74. Singh, L.P., *op. cit.*, pp. 14–15.
75. *Shillong Times,* April 1, 1998.
76. *Ibid.*
77. Singh, L.P., *op. cit.,* p. 16.
78. *Ibid.*, p. 17.
79. *Ibid.*
80. Namboodripad, E.M.S., *op. cit.,* p. 23.
81. *Ibid.*
82. *Ibid.*
83. *Ibid.*, p. 24.
84. The first theory is based mainly on William H. Riker's *Theory of Political Coalitions,* (New Haven, Yale University, 1962); and for the second theory by Abram de Swaan and Axelrod see Sridharan, E., "Coalition Politics", *Seminar* (New Delhi, No, 437, January 1996), p. 54 and Lijphart Arend, *Democracy in Plural Societies: A Comparative Exploration,* (Popular Prakashan, Bombay, 1989), Indian Reprint.
85. Riker, William H., *op. cit.,* (1962), p. IX.
86. Ibid., p. 13 comparing with writings of Von Neuman, John and Morgenstern, Oskar on *The Theory of Games and Economic Behaviour,* (Princeton University Press, 1944).
87. Riker, William H., *op. cit.,* (1962), p. 13.

88. *Ibid.*, pp. 16–20.
89. *Ibid.*, p. 75.
90. *Ibid.*, p. 102.
91. *Ibid.*, p. 103.
92. *Ibid.*, pp. 72, 74.
93. *Ibid.*, p. 104.
94. *Ibid.*, pp. 103–104.
95. *Ibid.*, pp. 102–104.
96. *Ibid.*, p. 185.
97. *Ibid.*, p. 211.
98. *Ibid.*
99. *Ibid.*
100. *Ibid.*, p. 243.
101. *Ibid.*, pp. 247–48.
102. Swaan, Abram de, *Coalition Theories and Cabinet Formations,* (Elsevier Scientific Publishing Company, Amsterdam, 1973), see *Encyclopaedia of Social Sciences,* (1977), Vol. 2, p. 529; also Sridharan, E., "Coalition Politics", *Seminar,* (New Delhi, No. 437, January 1996), pp. 53–57.
103. Sridharan, E., *op. cit., Ibid.*
104. Dahl, Robert A., *Polyarchy: Participation and Opposition,* (Yale University Press, (New Heaven, 1971), pp. 1–9; 231–49 cited in Lijphart, Arend, *op. cit.*, p. 4.
105. Lijphart, Arend, op. cit., Ibid.
106. Eckstein, Harry, *Division and Cohesion in a Democracy,* (Princeton University Press, Princeton, 1966), p. 34 cited in Lijphart, Arend, *op. cit.,* p. 4.
107. Lijphart, Arend, *op. cit., Ibid.*
108. *Ibid.*, p. 24.
109. *Ibid.*, p. 5.
110. *Ibid.*, p. 7.
111. *Ibid.*, p. 65.
112. *Ibid.*, p. 36.
113. *Ibid.*, p. 106.
114. *Ibid.*, p. 237.
115. *Ibid.*, p. 238.
116. *Ibid.*, p. 237.
117. *Ibid.*, p. 158.
118. Narain, Iqbal and Lal, Mohan, "Coalitional Politics, Nation Building and Administration: From Myths to Reality", *The Indian Journal of Public Administration,* Vol. XVII, No. 4, October–December, 1971.
119. *Ibid.*, p. 583.

120. *Ibid.*, p. 584.
121. *Ibid.*
122. *Ibid.*
123. *Ibid.*, p. 585.
124. *Ibid.*
125. *Ibid.*
126. *Ibid.*
127. *Ibid.*, p. 600.
128. *Ibid.*
129. Prasad, Mahendra, "Coalition and Minority Governments in India", *Politics India,* (New Delhi), Vol. I, No. 12, June 1997, p. 29.
130. *Ibid.*
131. *Ibid.*
132. *Ibid.*
133. *Ibid.*
134. *Ibid.*, citing Strom, Kaare, *Minority Government and Majority Rule,* (Cambridge University Press, 1990), p. 7.
135. Minocha, O.P., "Coalition Government—Experience and Prospects", Theme paper of the 40th Members' Annual Conference, October 27, 1996, Indian Institute of Public Administration, New Delhi, p. 2.
136. *Ibid.*
137. *Ibid.* pp. 3–4, Blakcwell's *Encyclopaedia of Political Institutions* (1987) used the term "kinds of coalition Governments" rather than patterns, levels or types; see Prasad, Mahendra, *op. cit.,* pp. 27–28.
138. Minocha, O.P., *Ibid.*, p. 2.
139. Chakravarty, Nikhil, "Coalition Politics and Impending Poll", *Mainstream,* (New Delhi, Vol. XXXV, No. 52, December 6, 1997, p. 3.
140. *Telegraph,* (Calcutta), March 15, 1998.
141. *Ibid.*
142. *Ibid.*
143. *Ibid.*
144. *Ibid.*
145. Narain, Iqbal and Lal, Mohan, *op. cit.*, p. 583.
146. *Ibid.*, p. 600.
147. *Ibid.*
148. *Ibid.*
149. *Ibid.*
150. Desai, A.R., *State and Society in India: Essays in Dissent,* (Popular Prakashan, Bombay, 1975), p. 179.
151. *Ibid.*

152. See Thandhavan, R., "Elections and Political Alliances in India", *The Indian Journal of Political Studies*, Vol. 12, December 1988, p. 23.
153. *Ibid.*, p. 24.
154. Bali, J.S., "The New Coalition Experiment: India Metamorphosis", *Politics India*, (New Delhi), Vol. I, No. 3, September 1996.
155. *Ibid.*, p. 57.
156. *Ibid.*
157. *Ibid.*
158. Desai, A.R., *op. cit.*, p. 173.
159. Prasad, Mahendra, *op. cit.*, pp. 27–28.
160. See *Monthly Public Opinion Surveys*, (India Institute of Public Opinion Pvt. Ltd., New Delhi), Vol. XLII, No. 1, October 1996, p. 4.
161. Riker, William H., in *Encyclopaedia of Social Sciences*, *op. cit.*, Vol. 6, p. 65.
162. *Ibid.*
163. *Ibid.*
164. *Ibid.*
165. Mehta, Balraj, "Coalition Politics: Meaningful and Responsive", *Monthly Public Opinion Surveys*, (India Institute of Public Opinion Pvt. Ltd., New Delhi), Vol. XLII, No. 8, May 1997, p. 25.
166. See *Monthly Public Opinion Surveys*, (India Institute of Public Opinion Pvt. Ltd., New Delhi), Vol. XLIII, No. 4, January 1998, p. 4.
167. Malik, S.C., "Coalition Governments: Perspective from Culture History", *Mainstream*, (New Delhi), Vol. XXVIII, No. 41, August 4, 1990, p. 29.
168. *Ibid.*, pp. 30, 35.
169. Pakem, B., "Party Government is a vital principle of a Representative government", *Meghalaya Legislative Assembly Silver Jubilee Souvenir* (1972–1997), p. 45; See also Achin Vanaik on "Coalition Politics", *Hindustan Times*, May 8, 1996.
170. Pakem, B., *op. cit.*, p. 45.
171. *Ibid.*
172. *Ibid.*
173. Ricks, Christopher, (ed.), *The Poems of Tennyson*, (Longmans, London, 1969), p. 697 "Locksley Hall" (1837–38), 11. 141–142.

DURING THE BRITISH PERIOD

1. Guha, Amalendu, *Planter Raj to Swaraj: Freedom Struggle and Electoral Politics in Assam, 1826–1947*, (Indian Council of Historical Research, New Delhi), 1977, p. 1.
2. Rao, V. Venkata and Hazarika, Niru, *A Century of Government and Politics in North-East India*, Vol. I, (Assam), 1874–1980, (S. Chand and Co., New Delhi), 1963, p. 102.
3. *Ibid.*, Guha gave 15 as the total membership, see Guha, A., *op. cit.*, p. 27.
4. Rao, V.V., and Hazarika, N., *op. cit.*, p. 103; Guha gave 42 as the total membership, see Guha, A., *op. cit.*, pp. 74–75.
5. Guha, A., *op. cit.*, pp. 78–79.
6. *Ibid.*, p. 79.
7. *Ibid.*, p. 81; See also Rao, V.V., and Hazarika, N., *op. cit.*, p. 103.
8. Guha, A., *op. cit.*, pp. 81, 83.
9. *Ibid.*, p. 83.
10. *Ibid.*, p. 121; See also Rao, V.V., and Hazarika, N., *op. cit.*, p. 103.
11. *Ibid.*
12. Guha, A., *op. cit.*, p. 148.
13. *Ibid.*, p. 157.
14. *Ibid.*, p. 160.
15. *Ibid.*, pp. 160–162
16. *Ibid.*, p. 190.
17. Rao, V.V., and Hazarika, N., *op. cit.*, p. 50.
18. *Ibid.*, p. 51.
19. *Ibid.*, p. 54.
20. *Ibid.*
21. *Ibid.*
22. *Ibid.*
23. *Ibid.*
24. *Ibid.*, p. 56.
25. *Ibid.*
26. *Ibid.*, p. 57.
27. Guha, A., *op. cit.*, p. 190; See also Rao, V.V., and Hazarika, N., *op. cit.*, p. 103.
28. Guha. A., *op. cit.*, pp. 219, 226.
29. Rao, V.V., and Hazarika, N., *op. cit.*, p. 60.

30. *Ibid.*, Guha gave February 5, 1938 instead of February 4, 1938. But the dates were in fact the same since Saadula had to continue until the new ministry was formed on February 5, 1938.
31. Guha, A., *op. cit.*, p. 217.
32. *Ibid.*, p. 221.
33. *Ibid.*, pp. 221, 226.
34. *Ibid.*, pp. 226, 229; See also Rao, V.V., and Hazarika, N., *op. cit.*, p. 62; and Borgohain, Munin Nath, *The Assam Legislative Assembly 1937–1962*, (Mrs. Annada Borgohain, Sibsagar), 1994, p. 277. The three accounts differed on the dates of the formation of the third coalition government led by G.N. Bordoloi. This had arisen due to the arrangement for a care-taker government of Saadula for about a week, that is, upto September 19 or 20, 1938.
35. Guha, A., *op. cit.*, p. 231; See also Rao, V.V., and Hazarika, N., *op. cit.*, p. 65; and Borgohain, M.N., *op. cit.*, p. 277.
36. Guha, A., *op. cit.*, pp. 231, 235; Rao and Hazarika, put it on November 15, 1939; and Borgohain put it on November 17, 1939.
37. Guha, A., *op. cit.*, p. 235; See also Rao, V.V., and Hazarika, N., *op. cit.*, p. 69.
38. Guha, A., *op. cit.*, p. 236.
39. *Ibid.*, p. 256.
40. *Ibid.*
41. *Ibid.*, pp. 265, 268.
42. *Ibid.*
43. *Ibid.*, pp. 268–69.
44. *Ibid.*, pp. 269–70; See also Rao, V.V., and Hazarika, N., *op. cit.*, p. 75.
45. Guha, A., *op. cit.*, pp. 271–72; Rao, V.V., and Hazarika, N., put August 19, 1942 as the date ending the third Saadula's coalition ministry though the date of Governor's Regime was put on August 24, 1942, See Rao, V.V., and Hazarika, N., *op. cit.*, p. 75.
46. Guha, A., *op. cit.*, pp. 273–281; Rao, V.V., and Hazarika, N., *op. cit.*, p. 82 gave the end of Saadula's fourth coalition ministry on March 22, 1945 though the date of the next coalition ministry was the same on March 24, 1945.
47. Guha, A., *op. cit.*, pp. 277, 280.
48. *Ibid.*, p. 281.
49. Rao, V.V., and Hazarika, N., *op. cit.*, p. 84.
50. *Ibid.*

51. Guha, A., *op. cit.*, pp. 279, 285.
52. Rao, V.V., and Hazarika, N., *op. cit.*, p. 84.
53. Guha, A., *op. cit.*, pp. 286–287.
54. Rao, V.V., and Hazarika, N., *op. cit.*, p. 84.
55. Guha, A., *op. cit.*, pp. 287–288.
56. *Ibid.*, pp. 288–289.
57. *Ibid.*, p. 289; Rao, V.V., and Hazarika, N., *op. cit.*, p. 84 gave the date of resignation as March 22, 1945 and the date of forming the new coalition government on March 24, 1945.
58. Guha, A., *op. cit.*, p. 289.
59. *Ibid.*, pp. 289–90.
60. *Ibid.*, p. 290.
61. *Ibid.*, p. 291.
62. *Ibid.*
63. *Ibid.*, pp. 303–305, 358.
64. *Ibid.*, pp. 303, 305, 310–311, 319, 337.
65. *Ibid.*, p. 320.
66. See Medhi, Kunja, *State Politics in India*, (Omsons Publications, Guwahati), 1988, p. 8.
67. *Ibid.*, p. 9.
68. Guha, A., *op. cit.*, p. 320, footnote 50.
69. *Ibid.*
70. *Ibid.*, p. 231.
71. *Ibid.*
72. *Ibid.*, pp. 231–32.
73. *Ibid.*, p. 232.

COALITION POLITICS IN NORTH-EAST INDIA SINCE INDEPENDENCE

1. Choudhury, J.N., *Arunachal Through Ages: From Frontier Tract to Union Territory*, (Jaya Choudhury, Shillong), 1984, pp. 218–228.
2. *Ibid.*, p. 233.
3. *Ibid.*, p. 235.
4. *Ibid.*, pp. 235–36.
5. *Ibid.*, pp. 240–42.
6. *Ibid.*, p. 317.
7. *Ibid.*, pp. 318–20; 335.
8. Talukdar, A.C., and Tado, Pura, "Assembly Elections in the North-East: A Case Study in Arunachal Pradesh", in Phukon, Girin and Yasin, Adil-ul, (eds.), *Working of Parliamentary Democracy and Electoral Politics in North-East*

India, (South Asia Publishers, New Delhi), 1998, p. 65.

9. See *Arunachal News,* Vol. 7, No. 6, October 1978, pp. 38–39.
10. Choudhury, J.N., *op. cit.,* pp. 336–338.
11. Talukdar, A.C., and Tado, Puro, *op. cit.,* p. 63.
12. *Ibid.,* p. 65.
13. *Ibid.,* pp. 66, 69.
14. Thomas, C.J., "Parliamentary Elections in Arunachal Pradesh", in Phukon, Girin and Yasin, Aditul, (eds.), *op. cit.,* p. 58.
15. Talukdar, A.C., and Yasin, Aditul, *op. cit.,* p. 72.
16. Borgohain, Munindra Nath, *The Assam Legislative Assembly (1937–1962),* (Mrs. Annada Borgohain, Sibsagar), 1994, p. 32.
17. *Ibid.*
18. *Ibid.*
19. *Ibid.*
20. *Ibid.*
21. Medhi, Kunja, *op. cit.,* p. 189.
22. Borgohain, Munindra Nath, *op. cit.,* p. 33.
23. Medhi, Kunja, *op. cit.,* p. 190.
24. *Ibid.,* 191.
25. *Ibid.,* pp. 191–192.
26. *Ibid.,* p. 192.
27. *Ibid.,* p. 32.
28. Rao, V. Venkata and Hazarika, Niru, *A Century of Government and Politics in North-East India,* Vol. I (Assam), 1974–1980, (S. Chand and Co., New Delhi) 1983, p. 86.
29. Medhi, Kunja, *op. cit.,* p. 48, footnote 5.
30. *Ibid.*
31. *Ibid.,* p. 48.
32. Rao, V. Venkata and Hazarika, Niru, *op. cit.,* p. 99.
33. Murty, T.S., *Assam: The Difficult Years: A Study of Political Developments in 1979–83,* (Himalayan Books, New Delhi), 1983, p. 2.
34. *Ibid.*; and Rao, V. Venkata and Hazarika, Niru, *op. cit.,* p. 99.
35. Rao, V. Venkata and Hazarika, Niru, *op. cit.,* pp. 93–94.
36. Murty, T.S., *op. cit.,* pp. 3–7.
37. *Ibid.,* p. 2.
38. *Ibid.,* p. 7.
39. *Ibid.,* pp. 7–8.
40. *Ibid.,* p. 8.
41. *Ibid.*

42. *Ibid.*
43. *Ibid.*, p. 10.
44. Cited in *Ibid.*
45. *Ibid.*, p. 12.
36. Rao, V. Venkata and Hazarika, Niru, *op. cit.*, p. 100, where they have mentioned PTCA with four members, seven Independents and three others.
37. *Ibid.*, p. 11.
48. *Ibid.*, p. 12.
49. *Ibid.*
50. Rao, V. Venkata and Hazarika, Niru, *op. cit.*, p. 100.
51. Murty, T.S., *op. cit.*, pp. 12–21.
52. *Ibid.*, p. 28.
53. *Ibid.*, pp. 28–30.
54. *Ibid.*, p. 28.
55. *Ibid.*, pp. 29–30.
56. *Ibid.*
57. *Ibid.*
58. *Ibid.*, pp. 108–107; and Rao, V. Venkata and Hazarika, Niru, *op. cit.*, p. 101.
59. Murty, T.S., *op. cit.*, p. 107.
60. *Ibid.*, pp. 108–109.
61. *Ibid.*, pp. 131–132.
62. *Ibid.*, p. 133.
63. *Ibid.*; See also Rao, V. Venkata and Hazarika, Niru, *op. cit.*, p. 101. Where June 29, 1981 was the date of Taimur's resignation.
64. Murty, T.S., *op. cit.*, pp. 135–136.
65. *Ibid.*, p. 136.
66. *Ibid.*, p. 138.
67. *Ibid.*, p. 155.
68. *Ibid.*, p. 156.
69. *Indian Recorder*, (New Delhi), Vol. III, No. 24, June 10–16, 1996, p. 2040.
70. Baruah, A.K., "Assam Elections 1996: The Congress Debacle", in Phukan, Girin and Yasin, Adil-ul, *op. cit.*, p. 28.
71. Goswami, Sandhya, "Assam Lok Sabha Elections 1996: An Analysis", in Phukon, Girin and Yasin, Adil-ul, *op. cit.*, p. 38.
72. *Indian Recorder*, (New Delhi), Vol. III, No. 24, June 10–16, 1996, pp. 2038–2039.
73. *Ibid.*, Vol. V, No. 38, September 17–23, 1998, p. 3931.
74. Deb, Bimal J., and Lahiri, Dilip K., *Manipur Culture and Politics*, (Mittal Publications) Delhi, 1987, pp. 27–28.

75. *Ibid.*, pp. 28–32.
76. *Ibid.*, p. 36.
77. *Ibid.*, p. 37.
78. *Ibid.*, p. 50.
79. *Ibid.*, pp. 52–55.
80. *Ibid.*, p. 107.
81. *Ibid.*, pp. 114–115.
82. *Ibid.*, p. 116.
83. *Ibid.*, p. 117.
84. *Ibid.*, pp. 117–118.
85. Ray, Ashok Kumar, "Kuki National Assembly: Its Social Basis and Working in Manipur", in Gassah, L.S., *Regional Political Parties in North-East India*, (Osmons, Publications) New Delhi, 1992, p. 194.
86. Deb, Bimal J., and Lahiri, Dilip K., *op. cit.*, pp. 123, 230–231.
87. Ray, Ashok Kumar, *op. cit.*, p. 194.
88. *Ibid.*
89. Deb, Bimal J., and Lahiri, Dilip K., *op. cit.*, p. 238.
90. *Ibid.*, p. 124.
91. *Ibid.*
92. *Ibid.*
93. *Ibid.*
94. *Ibid.* p. 126.
95. Choube, Shibanikinkar, *Hill Politics in North-East India*, (Orient Longman) Calcutta, 1973, p. 189.
96. Singh, Ravindra Pratap, *Electoral Politics in Manipur: A Spatio-Temporal Study*, (Concept Publishing Co.) New Delhi, 1981, pp. 22–23.
97. *Ibid.*, p. 27
98. *Ibid.*, pp. 23, 27.
99. *Ibid.*, p. 24.
100. *Ibid.*, p. 28.
101. *Ibid.*, pp. 31–32.
102. *Ibid.*, p. 36.
103. *Ibid.*, p. 85.
104. *Ibid.*, p. 37.
105. *Ibid.*, p. 40.
106. *Ibid.*, p. 44.
107. *Ibid.*, p. 86.
108. *Ibid.*, p. 87.
109. *Ibid.*, p. 94.
110. *Ibid.*, p. 95.
111. *Ibid.*, pp. 174–175.

112. *Ibid.*, p. 175.
113. *Ibid.*
114. *Ibid.*
115. *Ibid.*, p. 176.
116. *Ibid.*, p. 177.
117. *Ibid.*
118. *Ibid.*, p. 179.
119. *Ibid.*, pp. 180, 182.
120. *Ibid.*, p. 183.
121. *Ibid.*, pp. 184–185.
122. *Ibid.*, pp. 185–186.
123. *Ibid.*, pp. 187–188.
124. *Ibid.*, pp. 190–191.
125. *Asian Recorder* (New Delhi), Vol. XXXI, No. 5, January 29-February 4, 1985, p. 18156; See also Butler, David; Lahiri, Ashok and Roy, Prannoy (eds.) *India Decides: Elections 1952–1995,* (Books and Things) Delhi, 1995, p. 241, where they gave Congress with 29 members and 22 Independents.
126. *Asian Recorder,* (New Delhi), Vol. XXXVI, No. 15, April 9–15, 1990, p. 21094 and compare with the figures given by Butler, David, et.al., *op. cit.*, p. 241.
127. *Asian Recorder,* (New Delhi), Vol. XXXVI, No. 15, April 9–15, 1990, p. 21094.
128. *Ibid.*
129. *Indian Recorder,* (New Delhi), Vol. II, No. 3, January 15–21, 1995, p. 877.
130. *Indian Recorder,* (New Delhi), Vol. II, No. 7, February 12–18, 1995, p. 943.
131. *Ibid.*, Vol. II, No. 32, August 6–12, 1995, p. 1343; and Butler, David, et al., *op. cit.* p. 241.
132. *Indian Recorder,* (New Delhi), Vol. II, No. 7, February 12–18, 1995, p. 1343.
133. *Ibid.*
134. *Ibid.*, Vol. II, No. 37, September 10–16, 1995, p. 1421.
135. *Ibid.*, Vol. II, No. 41, October 8–14, 1995, p. 1485.
136. *Ibid.*, Vol. II, No. 52, December 24–31, 1995, p. 1661.
137. *Ibid.*, Vol. V, No. 4, January 22–28, 1998, p. 3389.
138. Lyngdoh, R.S., *Government and Politics in Meghalaya,* (Sanchar Publishing House), New Delhi, 1996, p. 468.
139. *Ibid.*, p. 343.
140. *Ibid.*, p. 460.
141. *Ibid.*, p. 450.
142. *Ibid.*, p. 471.

143. *Ibid.*, p. 450.
144. *Ibid.*, p. 461.
145. *Ibid.*
146. *Ibid.*, p. 464.
147. Rao, V. Venkata; Pakem, Barrister; and Hazarika, Niru, *A Century of Government and Politics in North-East India*, Vol. II (Meghalaya), 1874–1983, (S. Chand and Co.), New Delhi, 1984, p. 121.
148. *Ibid.*
149. *Ibid.*, p. 124.
150. *Ibid.*
151. *Ibid.*
152. *Ibid.*, p. 125.
153. *Ibid.*, p. 126.
154. *Ibid.*, p. 127; See also Malngaing, Pascal, "Electoral Politics in Meghalaya: A Study of the Meghalaya Federation and the Congress Party in the 1993 Elections", in Phukon, Girin and Yasin, Adil-ul, *op. cit.*, p. 88; and *The Election Archives*, (New Delhi), Vol. 19, No. 137–38, January–February, 1988, p. 84.
155. Rao, V. Venkata, et al., *op. cit.*, p. 128.
156. *The Election Archives*, (New Delhi), Vol. 19, No. 137–38, January–February, 1988, p. 84.
155. Rao, V. Venkata, et al., *op. cit.*, p. 128.
156. *The Election Archives*, (New Delhi), Vol. 19, No. 137–38, January–February, 1988, pp. 87–88.
157. *Ibid.*, pp. 92–94.
158. Sengupta, Susmita, "Political Coalition in Meghalaya: Meghalaya United Parliamentary Party (MUPP)", in Phukon, Girin and Yasin, Adil-ul, *op. cit.*, pp. 205–206.
159. *Ibid.*, p. 207; See also *Asian Recorder*, (New Delhi), Vol. XXXVII, No. 48, November 26–December 1, 1991, pp. 22026–27.
160. *Asian Recorder*, (New Delhi), Vol. XXXVIII, No. 11, March 11–17, 1992, pp. 22187–88.
161. Butler, David., *et al., op. cit.*, p. 244.
162. *Indian Recorder*, (New Delhi), Vol.V, No.13, March 26–April 1, 1998, pp. 3532.
163. *Ibid.*, Vol. V, No. 15, April 9–15, 1998, pp. 3566–67.
164. Choube, S.K., *op. cit.*, p. 7.
165. Rao, V. Venkata; Thansanga; and Hazarika, Niru, *A Century of Government and Politics in North-East India*, Vol. III, Mizoram, (S. Chand and Co.), New Delhi, 1987, p. 6.
166. *Ibid.*, p. 100.

167. *Ibid.*, p. 42.
168. *Ibid.*, pp. 50–54; 275.
169. *Ibid.*, p. 275.
170. *Ibid.*
171. *Ibid*; See also Rao, V. Venkata and Hazarika, Niru, *op. cit.*, pp. 93–94.
172. Rao, V. Venkata, et al., (1987), *op. cit.*, p. 144.
173. *Ibid.*, p. 216.
174. *Ibid.*, pp. 94; 153.
175. Prasad, R.N., "Mizo National Front Party and its Activities", in Gassah, L.S. (ed.), *op. cit.*, p. 163.
176. Rao, V. Venkata, et al., (1987), pp. 92–93; 117.
177. *Ibid.*, pp. 94–95, 117.
178. *Ibid.*, pp. 95, 117.
179. *Ibid.*, pp. 95, 117, 253.
180. *Ibid.* pp. 252–53; See also Nunthara, C., *Mizoram: Society and Polity*, (Indus Publishing Co.), New Delhi, 1996, pp. 150–152.
181. Rao, V. Venkata, et al., (1987), *op. cit.*, p. 126.
182. *Ibid.*, 130; See also *Election Archives*, (New Delhi), Vol. 18, No. 133–134, September–October, 1987, pp. 1–2.
183. Rao, V. Venkata, et al., (1987), p. 163.
184. Prasad, R.N., *op. cit.*, p. 163.
185. *Ibid.*, pp. 163–164.
186. *Ibid.*, p. 164.
187. *Asian Recorder*, (New Delhi), Vol. XXXV, No. 9 February 26–March 4, 1989, p. 20456.
188. Lal, Shiv (ed.), *Election Archives and International Politics*, Vol. 24, Nos. 207–208, November–December, 1993, pp. 95–96.
189. *Meghalaya Guardian*, (Shillong), October 12, 1998.
190. Choube, S.K., *op. cit.*, p. 12.
191. *Ibid.*
192. *Ibid.*
193. *Ibid.*, pp. 14, 16.
194. *Ibid.*, p. 13.
195. *Ibid.*, p. 15.
196. *Ibid.*, p. 66.
197. *Ibid.*, p. 149.
198. *Ibid.*, pp. 150–151.
199. *Ibid.*, p. 151.
200. Kumar, B.B., "Regional Political Parties in Nagaland: An Appraisal", in Gassah, L.S., (ed.), *op. cit.*, p. 207.
201. *Ibid.*

202. Butler, David, et al., *op. cit.*, p. 251.
203. Kumar, B.B., *op. cit.*, p. 208
204. *Ibid.*
205. *Ibid.*, p. 209.
206. Ibid.; See also Singh, R.P., "Electoral Politics in Nagaland", In Dutta, P.S., (ed.), *Electoral Politics in North-East India*, (Omsons Publications), New Delhi, 1986, pp. 179–191.
207. Kumar, B.B., *op. cit.*, p. 209.
208. *Election Archives*, (New Delhi), Vol. 18, No. 133–34, September–October, 1987, p. 73.
209. *Ibid.*, p. 74.
210. Kumar, B.B., *op. cit.*, p. 209.
211. *Ibid.*, p. 210.
212. Butler, David, et al., *op. cit.*, p. 251.
213. *Ibid.*
214. *Ibid.*
215. *Ibid.*
216. *Ibid.*
217. *Indian Recorder*, (New Delhi), Vol. V, No. 10, March 5–11, 1998, p. 3485.
218. *Ibid.*, Vol. V, No. 11, March 12–18, 1998, p. 3501.
219. Roychoudhuri, Nalini Ranjan, "The Historical Past", in Gan Choudhuri, Jagadis, (ed.), *Tripura: The Land and its People*, (Leela Devi Publications, Delhi), 1980, p. 32.
220. *Ibid.*, p. 33.
221. Bhattacharya, Bani Kantha, "Pattern of Administrative Organisation", in Gan Choudhuri, Jagadis, op. cit., p. 50.
222. *Ibid.*
223. *Ibid.*
224. *Ibid.*, p. 51.
225. *Ibid.*, p. 52.
226. *Ibid.*
227. Roychoudhuri, Nalini Ranjan, *op. cit.*, p. 38.
228. *Ibid.*
227. *Ibid.*, p. 39.
230. Gan Choudhuri, Jagadis, *A Political History of Tripura*, (Inter India Publications), New Delhi, 1985, p. 69; See also Gan Choudhuri, Jagadis, "Politics of Elections in Tripura", in Dutta, P.S. (ed.), *op. cit.*, p. 197.
231. Choube, S.K., *op. cit.*, p. 189.
232. Gan Choudhuri, Jagadis, (ed.), *op. cit.*, p. 133.
233. Gan Choudhuri, Jagadis, in Dutta, P.S., (ed.), *op. cit.*, p. 198.

234. Bhattacharya, Bani Kantha, in Gan Choudhuri, Jagadis, (ed.), *op. cit.*, p. 53.
235. Choube, S.K., op. cit., p. 189; See also Gan Choudhuri, Jagadis, (1985) *op. cit.*, p. 70.
236. Choube, S.K. *op. cit.*, pp. 189–190.
237. Bhattacharya, Bani Kantha, in Gan Choudhuri, Jagadis, (1980), (eds.), p. 53.
238. Gan Choudhuri, Jagadis, (1985), *op. cit.* pp. 72–73; See also Gan Choudhuri, Jagadis, in Dutta, P.S., (ed.) *op. cit.*, p. 198.
239. Butler, David, et al., *op. cit.*, p. 293.
240. Gan Choudhuri, Jagadis, (1980), (ed.), pp. 133–134.
241. Choube, S.K., *op. cit.*, pp. 190–191; See also Bhattacharya, Bani Kantha in Gan Choudhuri, Jagadis, (1980), (ed.) p. 54.
242. Bhattacharya, Bani Kantha, In Gan Choudhuri, Jagadis, (1980), (ed.) p. 54.
243. Gan Choudhuri, Jagadis, in Dutta, P.S., (ed.), *op. cit.*, p. 202. See also Gan Choudhuri, Jagadis, (1985), *op. cit.*, pp. 73–74.
244. Gan Choudhuri, Jagadis, in Dutta, P.S., (ed.), *op. cit.*, p. 203.
245. *Ibid.*, pp. 203–204.
246. Gan, Choudhuri, Jagadis, "The Electoral System", in Gan Choudhuri, Jagadis, (1980), (ed.), *op. cit.*, p. 134. See also Singh, V.B., and Bose, Shankar, (eds.), *State Elections in India: Data Handbook on Vidhan Sabha Elections, 1952–85,* (Sage Publications), New Delhi, 1987, Vol. 3: *The East and North-East,* pp. 80–81.
247. *Election Archives,* (New Delhi), Vol. 19, No. 137–38, January–February, 1988, p. 104; See also Gan Choudhuri, Jagadis, in Dutta, P.S. (ed.), *op. cit.*, p. 204; and also Gan Choudhuri, Jagadis, (1985), *op. cit.*, p. 74.
248. Butler, David, et al., pp. 292–93; See also *Election Archives,* (New Delhi), Vol. 19, No. 137–38, January–February, 1988, p. 108.
249. Butler, David, et al., *op. cit.*, p. 292.
250. *Indian Recorder,* (New Delhi), Vol. V, No. 15, April 9–15, 1998, p. 3568.

BIBLIOGRAPHY

1. Borgohain, Munindra Nath, *The Assam Legislative Assembly 1937–1962,* (Mrs. Annada Borgohain, Sibsagar), 1994.
2. Butler, David; Lahiri, Ashok; and Roy, Prannoy, (eds.), *Indian Decides: Elections 1952–1995,* (Books and Things, Delhi), 1995.
3. Choube, Shibanikinkar, *Hill Politics in North-East India,* (Orient Longmans, Calcutta), 1973.
4. Choudhury, J.N., *Arunachal Through Ages: From Frontier Tract to Union Territory,* (Jaya Choudhury, Shillong), 1984.
5. Dahl, Robert A., *Polyarchy: Participation and Opposition,* (Yale University Press, New Haven), 1971.
6. Deb, Bimal J., and Lahiri, Dilip K., *Manipur Culture and Politics,* (Mittal Publications, Delhi), 1987.
7. Desai, A.R., *State and Society in India: Essays on Dissent,* (Popular Prakashan, Bombay), 1975.
8. Dutta, P.S. (ed.), *Electoral Politics in North-East India,* (Omsons Publications, New Delhi), 1986.
9. Eckstein, Harry, *Division and Cohesion in a Democracy,* (Princeton University Press, Princeton), 1966.
10. Ehrenberg, Victor, *The Greek State,* (Methuen and Co., London), 1974.
11. Gan Choudhuri, Jagadis, *A Political History of Tripura,* (Inter India Publications, New Delhi), 1980.
12. Gan Choudhuri, Jagadis, (ed.), *Tripura: The Land and its People,* (Leela Devi Publications, Delhi), 1980.
13. Gassah, L.S. (ed.), *Regional Political Parties in North-east India,* (Omsons Publications, New Delhi), 1992.

14. Guha, Amelendu, *Planter Raj to Swaraj: Freedom Struggle and Electoral Politics in Assam 1826–1947* (Indian Council of Historical Research, New Delhi), 1977.
15. Gupta, R.L., The Politics of Commitment, (Trimurti Publications, New Delhi), 1972.
16. Gupta, S.P., and Ramachandra, K.S., (eds.), *Myth and Reality,* (Agam Prakashan, Delhi), 1976.
17. Hammond, N.G.L., *A History of Greece upto 322 B.C.,* (Clarendon Press, Oxford, London), 1973, Reprinted.
18. Karunakaram, K.P., (ed.), *Coalition Governments in India: Problems and Prospects,* (Indian Institute of Advanced Studies, Shimla), 1975.
19. Kashyap, Subhash C., *The Politics of Defection: A Study of State Politics in India,* (National Publishing House, New Delhi), 1969.
20. Kashyap, Subhash C., *The Politics of Power: Defection and State politics in India,* (National Publishing House, New Delhi), 1975.
21. Kothari, Rajni, *Politics in India,* (Orient Longmans, New Delhi), 1970.
22. Lal, Shiv, (ed.), *Election Archives and International Politics,* Vol. 24, Nos. 207–208, November–December, 1993.
23. Lewis, W. Arthur, *Politics in West Africa,* (Allen and Unwin, London), 1965.
24. Lijphart, Arend, *Democracy in Plural Societies: A Comparative Exploration,* (Popular Prakashan, Bombay, 1989, India Reprint.
25. Lyngdoh, R.S., *Government and Politics in Meghalaya,* (Sanchar Publishing House, New Delhi), 1996.
26. Medhi, Kunja, *State Politics in India, (Omsons Publications, Guwahati),* 1988.
27. Mommsen, Theodor, *The History of Rome,* (Macmillan, London), 1904, Vol. IV.
28. Murty, T.S., *Assam: The Difficult Years: A Study of Political Development in 1979–83,* (Himalayan Books, New Delhi), 1983.
29. Nunthara, C., *Mizoram: Society and Polity,* (Indus Publishing Co., New Delhi), 1996.
30. Phukon, Girin and Yasin Adil-ul, (eds.), *Working of Parliamentary Democracy and Electoral Politics in North-East India,* (South Asia Publishers, New hi), 1983.
31. Rao, V. Venkata, and Hazarika, Niru, A Century of Government and Politics in North-East India, 1874–1980, Vol. I, (Assam), (S. Chand and Co., New Delhi), 1983.

32. Rao, V. Venkata; Pakem, Barrister; and Hazarika, Niru, *A Century of Government and Politics in North-East India,* Vol. II (Meghalaya), 1874–1983, (S. Chand and Co., New Delhi), 1984.
33. Rao, V. Venkata; Thansanga; and Hazarika, Niru, *A Century of Government and Politics in North-East India,* Vol. III, Mizoram, (S. Chand and Co., New Delhi), 1987.
34. Ricks, Christopher, (ed.), *The Poems of Tennyson,* (Longmans, London), 1969 on Locksley Hall (1837–38).
35. Riker, William H., *Theory of Political Coalitions* (Yale University, New Haven), 1962.
36. Sarkar, Khhimuddin, *Aspects of Historical Geography of Pragjyotisa Kamrup: Ancient Assam* (Naya Prakashan, Calcutta), 1992.
37. Singh, Ravindra Pratap, *Electoral Politics in Manipur—A Spatto-temporal Study,* (Concept Publishing Co., New Delhi), 1981.
38. Singh, V.B. and Bose, Shankar, (eds.), *State Elections in India: Data Handbook on Vidhan Sabha Elections 1952–1985,* (Sage Publications, New Delhi), 1987, Vol. 3: *The East and North-East.*
39. Strom, Kaare, *Minority Government and Majority Rule,* (Cambridge University Press), 1990.
40. Swaan, Abram de, *Coalition Theories and Cabinet Formations,* (Elsevier Scientific Publishing Co., Amsterdam), 1973.
41. Von Neuman, John and Morgenstern, Oskar, *The Theory of Games and Economic Behaviour,* (Princeton University Press), 1944.
42. Weiner, Myron, *Party Politics in India: The Development of a Multi-Party System,* (Princeton University Press), 1957.

B: ARTICLES

1. Bali, J.S., "The New Coalition Experiment: India Metamorphosis", in *Politics India,* (New Delhi), Vol. I, No. 3, September, 1996.
2. Baruah, A.K., "Assam Elections 1996: The Congress Debacle", in Phukon, Girin and Yasin Adil-ul, (eds.), *Working of Parliamentary Democracy and Electoral Politics in North-East India,* (South Asia Publications, New Delhi), 1998.
3. Bhattacharya, Bani Kantha, "Patterns of Administrative Organisation", in Gan Choudhuri, Jagadis, (ed.), *Tripura:*

The Land and its People, (Leela Devi Publications, Delhi), 1980.

4. Chakravarty, Nikhil, "Coalition Politics and Impending Poll", in *Mainstream,* (New Delhi), Vol. XXXV, No. 54, December 6, 1997.
5. Dandavate, Madhu, "Coalition Politics in India", in *Politics India,* (New Delhi), February 1997.
6. Gamson, William A., "Coalition Formation", in *Encyclopaedia of Social Sciences,* (MacMillan, New York), 1972, Reprint.
7. Gan Choudhuri, Jagadis, "Politics of Elections in Tripura", in Dutta, P.S., (ed.), *Electoral Politics in North-East India,* (Omsons Publications, New Delhi), 1986.
8. Gan Choudhuri, Jagadis, "The Electoral System", in Gan Choudhuri, Jagadis, (ed.), *Tripura: The Land and its People,* (Leela Devi Publications, Delhi), 1980.
9. Goswami, Sandhya, "Assam Lok Sabha Elections 1996: An Analysis", in Phukon, Girin, and Yasin, Adil-ul, (eds.), *Working of Parliamentary Democracy and Electoral Politics in North-East India,* (South Asia Publications, New Delhi), 1998..
10. Khare, Harish, "Coalition Politics", in *Seminar,* (New Delhi) No. 377, January 1991.
11. Kumar, B.B., "Regional Political Parties in Nagaland: An Appraisal", in Gassah, L.S., (ed.), *Regional Political Parties in North-East India,* (Omsons Publications, New Delhi), 1992.
12. Malik, S.C., "Coalition Governments: Perspective from Culture History", in *Mainstream,* (New Delhi), Vol. XXVIII, No. 41, August 1990.
13. Malngiang, Pascal, "Electoral Politics in Meghalaya: A Study of the Meghalaya Federation and the Congress Party in the 1993 Elections", in Phukon, Girin, and Yasin, Adil-ul, (eds.), *Working of Parliamentary Democracy and Electoral Politics in North-East India,* (South Asia Publications, New Delhi), 1998.
14. Mehta, Balraj, "Coalition Politics: Meaningful and Responsive", in *Monthly Public Opinion Surveys,* (Indian Institute of Public Opinion Pvt. Ltd., New Delhi), Vol. XLIII, No. 4, January 1998.
15. Minocha, O.P., "Coalition Government: Experience and Prospects", A Theme Paper during the 40th Members' Annual Conference of the Indian Institute of Public Administration, New Delhi, 1996 (unpublished).

16. Namboodripad, E.M.S., "Means to an End", in *Seminar,* (New Delhi), No. 298, July 1984.
17. Narain, Iqbal, and Lal, Mohan, "Coalition Politics, Nation Building and Administration: From Myth to Reality" in *The Indian Journal of Public* Administration, (New Delhi), Vol. XVII, No. 4, October–December, 1971.
18. Pakem, B., "Electoral Politics in North-East India and Development in Political Theory", in *Proceedings of the North-East India Political Science Association,* Sixth Annual Conference, Dibrugarh University, (Dibrugarh), December 1996.
19. Pakem, B., Party Government is a Vital Principle of a Representative Government", in *Meghalaya Legislative Assembly Silver Jubilee Souvenir,* (1972–1997).
20. Prasad, Mahendra, "Coalition and Minority Governments in India", in *Politics India,* (New Delhi), Vol. I, No. 12, June 1997.
21. Prasad, R.N., "Mizo National Front Party and its Activities", in Gassah, L.S., (ed.), *Regional Political Parties" in North-East India,* (Omsons Publications, New Delhi), 1992.
22. Ray, Ashok Kumar, "Kuki National Assembly: Its Social Basis and Working in Manipur", in Gassah, L.S., (ed.), *Regional Political Parties in North-East India,* (Omsons Publications, New Delhi), 1992.
23. Riker, William H., "The Study of Coalitions", in *Encyclopaedia of Social Sciences,* (MacMillan, New York), 1972, Reprint.
24. Roy, Ash Narain, "Stress and Consensus", in *Hindustan Times,* (New Delhi), April 2, 1998, Editorial page.
25. Roy Choudhuri, Nalini Rajan, "The Historical Past", in Gan Choudhuri, Jagadis, (ed.), *Tripura: The Land and its People,* (Leela Devi Publications, Delhi), 1980.
26. San, Mohit, "Coalition Politics", in *Politics India,* (New Delhi), March 1997.
27. Sengupta, Susmita, "Political Coalition in Meghalaya: Meghalaya United Parliamentary Party (MUPP)", in Phukon, Girin, and Yasin, Adil-ul, (eds.), *Working of Parliamentary Democracy and Electoral Politics in North-East India,* (South Asia Publications, New Delhi), 1998.
28. Singh, L.P., "Learning from Experience", in a *Coalition Future, Seminar* (New Delhi), No. 298, July 1984.
29. Singh, Raghuveer, "Coalition Politics: Some Considerations", in Karunakaran, K.P., (ed.), *Coalition Governments in India: Problems and Prospects,* (Indian Institute of Advanced Study, Shimla), 1975.

30. Singh, R.P., "Electoral Politics in Nagaland", in Dutta, P.S., (ed.), *Electoral Politics in North-East India*, (Omsons Publications, New Delhi), 1986.
31. Sridharan, E., "Coalition Politics, in *Seminar*, (New Delhi), No. 437, January 1996.
32. Talukdar, A.C., and Tado, Pura, "Assembly Elections in North-East: A Case Study in Arunachal Pradesh", in Phukon, Girin, and Yasin, Adil-ul, (eds.), *Working of Parliamentary Democracy and Electoral Politics in North-East India*, (South Asia Publications, New Delhi), 1998.
33. Thandhavan, R., "Elections and Political Alliances in India", in *The Indian Journal of Political Studies*, Vol. 12, December 1988.
34. Thomas, C.J., "Parliamentary Elections in Arunachal Pradesh", in Phukon, Girin, and Yasin, Adil-ul, (eds.), *Working of Parliamentary Democracy and Electoral Politics in North-East India*, (South Asia Publications, New Delhi), 1998.
35. Vanik, Achin, "Coalition Politics", in *Hindustan Times*, (New Delhi), May 8, 1996.

C: DICTIONARIES, ENCYCLOPAEDIA, JOURNALS AND NEWSPAPERS (SELECTED)

1. *Asia Recorder*, (New Delhi), Vol. XXXI, No. 5, January 29–February 4, 1985; XXXV, No. 9, February 26–March 4, 1989; XXXVI, No. 15, April 9–15, 1990; XXXVII, No. 48, November 26–December 1, 1991; XXXVIII, No. 11, March 11–17, 1992.
2. *Encyclopaedia Americana*, (New York), 1972, Vols. 2; 21.
3. *Encyclopaedia Britannica*, (London), 1973, Vol. 17.
4. *Encyclopaedia of Political Institutions*, 1987.
5. *Encyclopaedia of Social Sciences*, (MacMillan, New York), 1972, Vol. 7; 1977, Vol. 2.
6. *Hindustan Times*, (New Delhi), May 8, 1996; April 2, 1998.
7. *Indian Recorder*, (New Delhi), Vol. II, No. 3, January 15–21, 1995; No. 7, February 12–18, 1995; No. 32, August 6–12, 1995; No. 37, September 10–16, 1995; No. 41, October 8–14, 1995; No. 52, December 24–31, 1995; Vol. III, No. 24, June 10–16, 1996; Vol. V, No. 4, January 22–28, 1998; No.10, March 5–11, 1998; No. 11, March 12–18, 1998; No. 13, March 26–April 1, 1998; No. 15, April 9–15, 1998.

8. *Mainstream,* (New Delhi), Vol. XXVIII, No. 41, August 4, 1990; Vol. XXXV, No. 52, December 6, 1997.
9. *Meghalaya Guardian,* (Shillong), October 12, 1998.
10. *Meghalaya Legislative Assembly Silver Jubilee Souvenir,* (1972–1997).
11. *Monthly Public Opinion Surveys,* (Indian Institute of Public Opinion Pvt. Ltd. New Delhi), Vol. XLII, No. 1, October 1996, No. 8, May 1997; Vol. XLIII, No. 4, January 1998.
12. *Oxford English Dictionary,* (Clarendon Press, Oxford, London), 1961, Reprinted.
13. *Politics India,* (New Delhi), September 1996; February 1997; March 1997; June 1997.
14. *Random House of English Language,* (Tulsi Shah Enterprises, Bombay), 1970.
15. *Seminar,* (New Delhi), No. 248, July 1984; No. 377, January 1991; No. 437, January 1996.
16. *Shillong Times,* (Shillong), April 1, 1998.
17. *Telegraph,* (Calcutta), March 15, 1998.
18. *The Election Archives,* (New Delhi), Vol. 18, No. 133–134; September–October, 1987; Vol. 19, No. 137–138; January–February, 1988.
19. *The Indian Journal of Political Studies,* Vol. 12, December 1988.
20. *The Indian Journal of Public Administration,* (New Delhi), Vol. XVII, No. 4, October–December, 1971.